PROMOTING CREATIVITY IN CHILDHOOD

PROMOTING CREATIVITY IN CHILDHOOD

A Practical guide for counselors, educators, and parents

Nanolla Yazdani, Ph. D.

authorHOUSE®

AuthorHouse™
1663 Liberty Drive
Bloomington, IN 47403
www.authorhouse.com
Phone: 1-800-839-8640

First published by AuthorHouse   04/18/11

ISBN: 978-1-4567-6332-9-(sc)
ISBN: 978-1-4567-6331-2-(dj)
ISBN: 978-1-4567-6330-5 (ebk)

Library of Congress Control Number: Pending

Printed in the United States of America

Any people depicted in stock imagery provided by Thinkstock are models, and such images are being used for illustrative purposes only. Certain stock imagery © Thinkstock.

This book is printed on acid-free paper.

Because of the dynamic nature of the Internet, any web addresses or links contained in this book may have changed since publication and may no longer be valid. The views expressed in this work are solely those of the author and do not necessarily reflect the views of the publisher, and the publisher hereby disclaims any responsibility for them.

To my family
Lisa, Teryn, & Lillie

Contents

CHAPTER FOUR
PHYSICAL DEVELOPMENT IN INFANCY
& TODDLERHOOD

CHAPTER FIVE
COGNITIVE DOMAIN IN INFANCY & TODDLERHOOH

CHAPTER SIX
PSYCHOSOCIAL DEVELOPMENTIN INFANCY & TODDLERHOOD

CHAPTER SEVEN
PHYSICAL DEVELOPMENT IN EARLY CHILDHOOD

CHAPTER EIGHT
COGNITIVE DEVELOPMENT IN EARLY CHILDHOOD

CHAPTER NINE
EMOTIONAL DEVELOPMENT IN EARLY CHILDHOOD

OVERVIEW

How does the phenomenon of creativity and giftedness evolve in the people? Is it possible to nurture creativity and giftedness as early as the embryonic and infancy stages? *Promoting Creativity in Childhood* explains the dynamics of human development and the opportunities for enhancing creativity through embryonic, infancy and early childhood developmental stages. Furthermore, in this book we discuss the physical, cognitive, and psychosocial development of humans in three developmental phases: embryonic, infancy, and early childhood.

Designed specifically as a text book for undergraduate courses in gifted education, early childhood education, counseling and psychology *Promoting Creativity in Childhood* offers a broad overview of foundational principles and practical approaches for developing the creative potential of children at school and home. Though brief, this pragmatic text provides the materials suggested by accrediting bodies for basic guidance, teaching, and developing courses. This text offers insight into an array of important topics, including: The changes and continuity of life from day one in the womb until the end of 6 years of life.

Enhancing creativity is one of the main focuses of this book. The intention of this book is to explore the strategies for educators, counselors and parents, aimed at unlocking the creative potential in the first six years of life. The nine chapters are designed to improve knowledge, aid in educational and mental health planning, and facilitate parenting skills. Taking into consideration the physical, cognitive, and psychosocial developments of humans in the embryonic and the first six years of life, this book attempts to address the windows of opportunities for enhancing creativity and giftedness. Strategies

1

and activities are aimed at unlocking the creative potential of humans with respect to the notion of growth and maturity, safety, readiness, cross cultural sensitivity, and efficiency.

As a concerned individual, it is essential to provide for a child in order to equip her/him for the future. Nevertheless, the essence of this book is not embedded in the idea of introducing more competitiveness for future generations; rather, pioneering the happiness and successful attitude for the future citizens of this planet.

Promoting Creativity In Childhood will help educators, parents, caregivers, and counselors to have a deeper understanding of creativity as a natural function in the human species. Its strategies to nurture such potential in the embryonic phase and the first six years of life will add to the success and happiness of the children. It is responsible to say that the facilitative role of this book improves the intellectual, emotional, and psychosocial functioning of young children whom are the decision-makers of tomorrow. The utmost objectives of this book are sharing information, purposing activities and strategies, facilitating therapeutic sessions, and providing in depth guidance for early childhood educational settings.

The introduction chapter recounts a preliminary prologue to human development and some selected theoretical backgrounds for physical, cognitive-linguistic and psycho-social developments. The second chapter is devoted to the importance of early intervention, and creativity and giftedness from historical and operational perspectives. These two chapters set the stage for the introduction of related educational activities and practical propositions in the six upcoming chapters. These educational activities are designed to enhance the creative abilities with respect to physical, cognitive and the psychosocial domains in infants, toddlers, and preschoolers.

The intention is that this book will not only meet the rigorous demands of parents and educators but also provide a lively and dynamic overview for mental health professionals. *Promoting Creativity in Childhood* offers the advanced, practical, multicultural, and quality knowledge and research-based materials, which are simple to understand and original to apply. Most of the references in this book are the giants in the field of creativity, child development, education, and psychology. Each chapter has a relatively similar format.

Chapter One

HUMAN DEVELOPMENT

Introduction

How young do children learn? To what degree do the early experiences efficiently influence maturity and creativity in later age? Can early intervention sway creative potentials?

To answer these questions, one should first grasp the idea of human development. The hereditary characteristic that we acquire from our parents and the environment influences on what we will become. The field of developmental psychology basically looks at how and why people change or stay the same throughout the entire life-span. Therefore the essential role of learning can be explored as starting steps to the opening questions.

Based on the present scientific literatures learning starts in the womb. Further more, infancy and early childhood periods provide an irrefutable opportunity to unleash the creative potentials in human species. For the past fifty years, the researchers discovered that creative people are inclined to have average or above average scores on IQ tests, beyond an IQ of about 120 with modest correlation between creativity and intelligence. Additionally, the findings during this period reveal a fact that environment is more important than heredity in influencing creativity, and a child's creativity can be buoyant or dispirited by early experiences at home or school settings. Given what is known about human learning, how can the environment be modified to best support children's emerging creativity?

The characteristics of this amended and modified environment are based on the understanding of three general principles: time, space, and occasion. With respect to *time*, the reality is that creativity does not follow time. When creative forces are aligned to function, there are conscious or subconscious forces are in operation. In another word, there is no way to tell when the creative product or thought may come out of the incubation phase. Therefore, the timing for creative production does not follow the clock or calendar. On the contrary, *time* plays a decisive role in the development of creativity. Throughout the developmental phases of human growth, from embryo to old age, time plays a crucial factor in formation and production of creativity. However, time is also a very tricky factor when it comes to placing time limits for production of creative thoughts. Researchers have found that *time* has a negative effect of production of original verbal imagery, the main component of creative thought (Khatena, 1982 & Yazdani, 1984). With regard to *space*, creativity needs a favorable environment to be flourished and fostered. The atmosphere, whether it is a womb, a home or a class-room can reflect encouragement or discouragement. A climate of support and empowerment which elicit motivation, acceptance of mistake, risk-taking, and rich in emotional and cognitive stimulation can easily kindle a creative cycle. This creative cycle which starts with imagination and winds up with a novel and original thought or product is highly sensitive to *space* in which it incubates or manifests. In connection with *occasion*, creativity encounters an intense and a concentrated arousing between internal self and external world. The role of personality and the dynamics of the need-fulfillment of the individual play a vital role in the formation of creative imagination imagery. Creating an *occasion* to foster and regulate this need fulfillment process is in the hand of parents, teachers, and counselors. Therefore, the early interventions will positively expedite creativity.

For centuries the growth and the development of humans were the subject of many philosophers and scientists. Many different attributions of growth have been used as the criterion for the overall explanation of the development of our species. But in recent years, most developmental psychologists decided to look at the human growth and development from the following stand points: physical, cognitive and linguistic, psychosocial domains. In our species, we go through several distinct developmental phases which are entirely differentiated from each others, embryonic, fetus, infancy, early childhood, pre-adolescence, and adulthood. These phases are differentiated from each other with regard to the content, structure, and function. Each phase has its own capacity to interact with the environment and gain mastery of its related skills. After gaining necessary skills to interact with environment, the organism moves to the next developmental phase. It is important to know that there are group of people move across these developmental phases without gaining adequate mastery of skills for that particular developmental phase. Consequently, few of these individual will adapt, but simply most of them fall behind.

Never the less, gaining mastery in each phase requires adequate execution of its function and maturity of its structure which leads to the gaining a necessary skills to function appropriately for that phase. There is no secret that maturity of the function and the readiness of the structure for a healthy transition to the next phase have a direct correlation with an enriched environment. Therefore, it is logical to say the early interventions promote the healthy and necessary patterns of skills and traits to facilitate the advanced physical, cognitive/linguistic, and psychosocial growth of a child. For every child, the first six years of life is a budding period in terms of perceptual skills, cognitive and emotional development, with respect to creativity. Primarily, many children are lost during this budding time as a consequence of inadequate stimulation and poor timely intervention. The fact that all children need and profit from loving and encouraging environment in the early phase of life (Sellin & Birch, 1980), remains undisputed.

How often have we heard that the practice of nurturing the potential of children has been the sole responsibility of parents? However, in the modern days this responsibility has been shared with the other professionals in different sectors, besides parents, educators, and mental health professionals who are deeply involve with accountability of nurturing the children and up bringing their developmental skills. Consider, for a moment, what a person, who was exposed to reasonable and well designed intervention strategies in early part of life, can do. Knowing this person's life, a product of many strands, beyond a shadow of a doubt, this individual had developed his/her potentials to the point that can understand his or her universe in a unique way. Now, the big question is, how much of this person's potential, as a human being, is provided or limited by hereditary or environment?

What is Child Development?

Child development is defined as a scientific study of the patterns of growth, change, and stability that transpire from conception through the adolescence (Feldman, 2007). Referring to a common approach to human development, by it self, the notion of *change* and *continuity* throughout the life of human is called *"development"*. This growth and expansion is sometimes subject to total change in function or assimilation in efficacy. This blend of changes and continuities are going to be studied from three developmental perspectives or *domains* (Seifert & Hoffnung, 2000) known as *physical domain, cognitive domain* and *psychosocial domain.*

Physical development refers to permanence and changes related to growth, motor skills, and sensory perception. Cognitive development explains the relationship between physical growth of organism, changes related to thinking, learning, memory, language development, creativity and intellectual capabilities. Psychosocial developments submit to stability and change in the enduring characteristics that differentiate one person from the others, social knowledge, identity arrangement, self concept, feelings and mode of the interactions with self and others.

The appropriate maturity in the composition of these domains, in each developmental phase, leads to healthy evolution to the next developmental phase. There are two major clusters of developmental theories. One group of developmental psychologists are of the opinion that each phase of the development has its own structure and function and intervention above the capacity of that particular phase is not only detrimental, but it is almost impossible. On the contrary, the majority of the scientists believe that the mind is capable of learning at any given time, if the proper intervention were applied. In this book we discuss the physical, cognitive, and psychosocial development of human in three developmental phases: embryonic, infancy, and early childhood. The changes and continuity of life from day one in the womb until the end of 6th years of life is the subject of inquiry.

Historical Perception of Children

The interest of society on the progress and survival of its people has been the center of attention for millenniums. Transferring its heritage, whether it was tradition, culture, language, wealth, or anything else was always trusted to a few capable individuals. Certain characteristics have been the ear mark of these trusted persons which one is intelligent. Therefore, training and empowering, in another word developing, the children to carry out different tasks has been the focus of generations. The first historical landmark in child development comes from a written documentation China.

Around 5000 to 4000 B.C. in ancient China, the royal families were interested in the intellectual development of children who are supposed to become the future government workers. From that point on, the next written documentation pertaining to a child's development came from Hippocrates, a Greek physician who classified human personality. According to Hippocrates some children, with more yellow bile than others were easily angered; others, with excess blood, were more cheerful; and so on. Since Hippocrates, history has not been able to record any information about child development until the Medieval Times.

In Western societies, children were not regard as young people until the past several hundred years. In other words, there was a time that childhood did not exist! Before 1600 A.D., during medieval times, an infant was regarded as only a talented pet. They were considered as miniature adults; by the way they were dressed, carrying responsibility as a caregiver for younger siblings or even work in the farms. In the 1700s in Germany, parents started to show interests in the growth of their child by recording physical and linguistic milestones in their child's life. Another landmark in child development can be credited to the work of Rousseau in 1762 with publication of "Emile" regarding to formal discipline of children. This writing inspired the first real scientific observation of an infant by a Swiss educator, Johann Heinrich Pestalozzi, who started a new trend: Parents as scientists.

Nevertheless, the early contribution of thinkers indicates that the philosophical thinking of the seventeen century, influenced by John Locke, the founder of *empiricism,* stated that an infant's mind is a *Tabula Rasa* (a blank tablet) on which the environment makes its impression through knowledge and experience. Additionally this American educator, Locke, 1892 purposed a monumental piece of work "Some Thoughts Concerning Education". This work for the first time encountered "Delight in Discovery". This opened a door for influence of educators out side of house. In eighteen century, David Hume was concurring with Locke that the environment was the only imperative component in determining the child's development. It is important to know that in those days, the belief was, that mental events were only impressions or sensations, and more complicated behaviors such as reasoning, judgment, and thinking came from replication of impressions and sensations. This position was totally rejected by Locke that physiology was the only element in thinking process of human.

Another monumental thinking, influenced modern theories of learning came from Germany. On the other hand the German philosopher, Immanuel Kant, purposed during the eighteenth century an idea that people have their own built-in instincts or "natural purposes". Kant's theory was the first to focus on the instinctive capability of humans. In his way of thinking, these "innate capabilities" use the surrounding environment to grow and survive.

In France, during the eighteenth century, another interesting train of thought known as existentialism developed. Jean Jacques Rousseau, an existentialist, explained that infants and children are equipped with the instinctive capability to understand the difference between right and wrong. He believed this "intuitive" sense directs the child throughout stages of development.

It was not until the discovery of the Austrian monk, George Mendel, what we call today a *chromosomes & genes*; the role of hereditary and environment became separated. By the final touch of Darwin in 19th century, the debate of heredity and environment was taken to a new level of scientific endowment. The first scientific work in the field of child development started with the work of Charles Darwin; he started to see a child as a good derivation for studying the adult. The two trends of thought that stated man is inactive, proposed by Locke and Hume, in contrast with Kant, Rousseau, and Darwin's ideas that people take an active role in their own development; a new beginning emerged.

Perhaps the most profound influence on developmental psychologist was two ideas of getting information about a child should come from the child and the concept of adolescence. The credit for these two monumental ideas goes to the first developmental psychologist, G. Stanley Hall (1844-1924).

The next important landmark in the new area of scientific approach to the child development could be credited to the extensive work of Pavlov in Russia, Skinner and Watson in the United States, Piaget in Switzerland, and Freud in Austria. These giants of behavioral science opened the door to a better understanding of human behavior by introducing rewarding principles, distinctive period of development, and role of consciousness. Additionally, in the 20th century several figures became the center of attention in child development with respect to cognitive domain. Among those contributors we can name Binet in France, intelligence testing for children; Hollingsworth, first psychologist focusing on child development; Stanford in 1920 with his study on gifted children; and Wechsler in 1949 with his contribution to defining intelligence.

Looking at the notion of creativity and its role in human development, particularly children, the work of several internationally known scientists from United States opened the door to the technical and systematic understanding of this field. Guilford and Torrance in mid 20th century, Khatena in 1970s and 1980s, Clark in 1980 and 1990s, and Weisberg in 21st century are considered as the forerunners of this modern area. The extensive work of these psychologists brought a greater vitality to the development of children with regard to the structure of intellect, creative thinking, imagination imagery, and role of emotion and cognition in creativity.

Since the explosion of research in creativity (Weisberg, 2006) and developmental psychology in the late part of 20th and early segment of 21st centuries; still the fundamental issue of hereditary and environmental influences remains the same: Is the child's physical growth, cognitive and creative functioning, personality and socialization performances are the product of heredity (biology) or environment (experience). Consequently, the periods of infancy and childhood, like the rest of life span of human are greatly influenced by the ongoing interaction between these two major factors; biology and environment. In today's view, the boundary of biology and environment determine the elicited behavior and the attempt to separate these two factors, will lead to a great error (Weisberg, 2006). Consequently, the central focus is the issue of *how much* and *in what way* the elicited behavior resulted from the influences of biological or environmental factors. Recently, a group of developmental psychologist looks at the role of socio-cultural influences on the human behavior. Nevertheless, the authenticity of socio-cultural impact on human growth has become the subject of many research in the early part of 21st century.

Theories and Perspectives of Human Development

What fuels the human behavior and action? The main attempt in this section is to understand the different views and perspective, explaining the manifestation of human action with respect to cognitive, but mainly emotive domains. Basically, change or development occurs within a specific stage until experience or maturation takes the organism to another stage (Cunningham, 1993). Generally, the long term changes taking place through the life span of human and the blueprints of these changes is regarded as *human development*. Knowing this important point that the developmental psychology is not a collection of cultural insight; it is a science (Craig & Dunn, 2007), the long term changes in human should be empirically evaluated. Due to the complexity of human behaviors, it is imperative to mention that no theory by itself has been able to explain the total ramification of these behaviors. Rather, it is safe to say that each theory has been able to shade a light on a sector or sectors of human behavior. For the purpose of this book we discuss only four distinct major perspectives about human development, biological, psychodynamic and its related, behavioral, and cognitive theories. It is valuable to know that each of these theories or perspectives were able to expand on a certain aspect of human, particularly child's development better than the others.

Therefore, collectively, these perspectives can shade a better light on the total understanding of human development.

Biological perspectives

In these views the origin of human behaviors are considered to be a biological descent. Biological theories have an emphasis on heredity and genetic bases for behavior. When the organism navigates through certain steps by the genetic order, certain maturation takes place and person move to another phase. This maturation takes place from head to tail (up to bottom) and inside outward. With respect to this view, human behavior is only driven by biological trigger and no other factor can activate the behavior. The logic behind such a perspective lays in the idea that since human is a biological organism; the elicited behaviors are influenced by physiological utilities.

One of the early biological perspective or theory is *Darwin's evolution theory* which explains the process through which species transform across generations. At the heart of this theory, the idea of *"natural selection"* rests on the fact that the individuals with better coping and adapting capabilities to the environment live longer to reproduce, *"survival of spices"*. The other biological base theory is *etiology theory*, which stresses the function of biological mechanism during infancy and early childhood on human development. This theory mostly concerns how certain behavioral and psychological traits that emerged extensively between human beings may have been instrumental in evolutionary survival of human species (Ainsworth & Bowlby, 1991). Instinctual behavioral patterns such as sucking, grasping in infant and attachment in infant and toddlers are among these evolutionary traits.

With the explosion of *neuroscience* in 1990s the connectivity of brain function and visible behaviors dominated the developmental psychology literatures. The research in the field of association between brain and human behavior particularly memory open a door in deeper understanding of the influence of brain tasks on behaviors and human development (Hayne, Boniface, & Barr, 2000) and possible association between evolutionary survival traits.

Psychodynamic and its Related Perspective

In this particular view the development of human personality was uniquely explained by means of the importance of unconsciousness. The value and the role of unconscious in formation of personality through the human life span and its role in personality triads and characteristics are best explained through this perspective. Sigmund Freud as a forerunner of the psychodynamic view expressed the idea that the human development are determine by unconsciousness which originated in human mind. The importance of early childhood experiences, especially with their caregiver plays an important role in formation of human personality. The interplay of three parts of personality; *id, ego, and superego*, determines the pattern of human feeling and to great extend, human cognition. The core of this idea reveals the point that the constant battle between ways of dealing with conflicts involving id impulses and ego as a rational problem-solving device spark the way human operates on conscious and unconscious levels. To protect itself, ego creates a pattern of functioning, known as *defense mechanism*, an unconscious deformation of reality which keeps away the pain from consciousness. This dynamic is occasionally in interaction with superego, the moral mind.

In view of the fact that social development is a part of the developmental constellation of human growth, the deeper understanding of three components of personality becomes imperative. *Id* impulse motivates the individual to either seek pleasure or avoid pain. *Ego* is mainly rational and conscious problem-solving machinery. Plus, *superego* is the moral and ethical module of personality. Given that the human development is viewed as the movement through stages such as oral, annual, phallic, latency, and genital, the resolution of each stage sets the frame for later development (Craig & Dunn, 2007). Table 1.1 presents the five Freudian psychosexual stages.

Psychosexual Stage	Description	Age
Oral	Gratification takes place through mouth	Birth to 18 months
Anal	Bodily interest is focused on anal region	18 months to 3 years

Phallic	Genital region is sector of gratification	3 to 6 years
Latency	Period of relative quiet. Focus is on gender-appropriate behaviors	6 years to puberty
Genital	Attention shifts from parents to peer. Sexual interests mature.	Puberty through adulthood

Table 1.1 Freudian Psychosexual Stages

The other important theory is relation to psychoanalysis is the psychosocial stages and developmental process of Erikson. In this view the process of psychosocial development of human is entrenched in the interaction between internal psychological factors and external environmental dynamics such as biological, life conditions, developmental history; and particular social, cultural influences. There are eight distinct psychosocial crisis stages and resolution in each stage facilitates the further movement to another stage. There are only two options in this process of movement from one stage to the other success or failure (Erikson, 1968).

1. Trust versus Mistrust: In this stage, approximate age birth to one year, the psychosocial calamities involves between trusting self and trusting the relationship with caregiver. This stage develops the notion of "hope".
2. Autonomy versus Shame: This stage, around age one to three years, focuses on the issue of controlling actions, thoughts and feeling by themselves. This stage is instrumental in developing the concept of "will".
3. Initiative versus Guilt: This stage, approximately age three to six years, centers on developing the ability to initiate verbal and physical activities. In this stage ability to explore and purposeful pursue of activity become the core of focus. This phase is influential in developing of "purpose".
4. Industry versus Inferiority: This stage, roughly age six to twelve, focuses on mastery, productivity, competence, and

development of capacity for positive self—concept. This stage is influential in developing of "competence".

5. Identity versus Role confusion: In this stage, approximately age twelve to nineteen, spotlight is on developing a reliable and integrated sense of who they are with emphases on prototype of self-concept. This phase is instrumental in rising of "fidelity".

6. Intimacy versus Isolation: This stage, roughly age nineteen to twenty five, point up on developing achievement of an intimate relationship and career track. This stage is influential for developing of "love".

7. Generativity versus Stagnation: This stage, approximately age of twenty five to fifty, focuses on creativity, personal satisfaction, and social meaningfulness. This stage aids of "care".

8. Ego integrity versus Despair: This stage, approximately age fifty and older focuses on belief of integrity of life, optimism and wisdom. This stage facilitates of "wisdom".

Behavioral perspectives

In this view the emphasis is centered on how the consequences of some behaviors influence behavior itself. Basically, any behavior that is reinforced is more likely to occur again in future. In these theories, the quality of observation and measurement of overt behavior are the only way to assess the behavior. Subjective notions such as mind, unconscious or feelings do not play any role in this line of theories. In other words what is important in this perspective is observable *behaving*. As the result of this line of initiatives, theories such as classical conditioning, operant conditioning begin to emerge. Pavlov (1849-1936) introduced the association-and-meaning learning known as *classical conditioning*. In classical conditioning the stimuli is subject to manipulation; where unconditioned stimulus is paired with conditioned stimuli and gradually the conditioned stimuli elicits conditioned response.

There is another conditioning theory known as trial-and-error learning or Operant Conditioning. In *operant conditioning*, the response is subject to manipulation. J. B. Skinner (1904-1990) introduced a new and widely used concept of operant conditioning. In this form of conditioning, the occurrence of desirable behaviors is reinforced immediately; by adding or removing a reinforcer whenever the desirable response is revealed. The reinforcement can be positive, negative, or manifests in the form of punishment.

Additionally, series of behaviorally oriented perspectives introduced the notion of modeling in human learning; known as theories is social learning. The *Social learning theory* views learning as a result of the influence of the social imitating of the behavior of others, through modeling and playing. Principally, all learning happens with reference to other people. Albert Bandura is credited to the promotion of this line of theories. Since the anticipated consequences of the behavior can be best learned in the social context, the children who are subject to this form of learning at home or school can greatly profit from this perspective.

Cognitive Perspectives

In general, cognitive perspective stresses on the process of thinking, reasoning and problem-solving. There are number of cognitive theories of development. The two most prominent one are Jean Piaget and Lev Vygotsky These two theories will be extensively discussed based on their contributions to the child development. In cognitive theories the emphasis on development is in the way a child thinks and on child's dealings with animate and inanimate surroundings.

Piaget's theory is a stage theory. Each stage built on what came before and provided the base for what will follow (Cunningham, 1993). Piaget argues that mind changes based on two principles, assimilation and accommodation. Also this growing mind cultivates and adapts to the world as the individual goes through different life cycles, with one huge limitation. Piaget believed that each life cycle or phase has its own capacity and structure which limits the child ability to operate beyond that capacity or parameters (Piaget, 1975). In another word the child has the capability to learn which is locked into the ability of that particular age bracket. To day a great number of developmental psychologists truly believe that this is a weakness of Piaget theory and child, in did can perform outside of these parameters.

However, understanding the theory of Piaget is essential in finding ways to accelerate the cognitive and emotive growth of the child with respect to creativity. Piaget believes each human goes through four distinct stages of cognitive development which is unique and specified for that particular stage. Each stage has its own structure and contents which allow the child to interact accordingly with the environment. Piaget stages of cognitive development divides to four stages:

I.   *Sensorimotor Stage:* Approximately age 0-2 years. In this stage infant starts to develop object permanence, where things in the world exist even if they can't be seen. In this stage infant learns through utilization of senses; particularly motor development, vision, and hearing. Intelligence relies on body motion, reflexes and sensory inputs.

II. *Preoperational Stage:* Roughly age 2-7. In this stage child starts to develop language and symbolic thinking and also the child become the center of his/her universe. The child understands the surrounding based on one or maximum two perspectives or dimensions. Utilization of symbolism through language and fascination with "magical" concept of cause and effect plays a very vital role in further cognitive development of the child.

XI. *Concrete Operational Stage:* Around age 7-11 or12 years. In this stage the of development the child begin to expand abilities in conservation, the idea that quality is unrelated to physical appearances, logical thinking start to emerge, explores the world and object based on several perspectives or dimensions.

XII. *Formal Operational Stage:* About age 11 or 12 years and up. The adolescent develops full logical thinking pattern with ability to guess and predict based on abstract thinking. The thinking become systematic and pays a lot of attention to possibilities rather than concrete thinking. Reasoning and analogy develops hand in hand at this phase.

Each of these four stages of development, known as *schemes*, has its own structure and content which process information accordingly (Seifert & Hoffnung, 2000). Learning takes place due to two processes of *assimilation* and *accommodation* which jointly leads to adaptation, a process by which organism changes to honor the environmental in put and formation of realities.

Another monumental perspective in the development of cognition is a theory, embedded in social context. In this theory the role of social interaction in formation of language as a symbolic tool in the development of cognition shows the importance of social and communal contacts. *Vygotsky social-cognitive theory* brings up an important point, human is a social being. When a child plays and socially interacts with others, it leads to a tremendous amount of learning. Vygotsky (1896-1934) was among the first to testify to the role of social context in children learning. He believed that learning is a shared venture which transferred through cognition and language. The higher mental functioning cultivates out of communal interactions and dialogue that takes place between child and other adults who are a part of child's life. In his idea of gradual integration of language and thoughts, Vygotsky explains that early speech is learned with little understanding of language and the child's connection between language and thought is the beginning of the establishment of his/her cognitive development (Seifert & Hoffnung, 2000). This principle simply testifies to the importance of constant, early contact with children.

Chapter two

CREATIVITY

New foundation

Creativity is a journey, starting with imagination and winding up with a product. Since the beginning of mankind the concept of creativity has been expressed in many different ways. Frankly, creativity is probably the only universal human trades. From the painting of *Bellowing Bison* in a Paleolithic cave in Altamira, Spain to the images of Hubble telescopes from space gazing to the far corners of universe, the notion of creativity has captured our imagination and fueled our curiosity. This universal human trait has been proved to be the most primitive core of our existence. It has given us the unique identity as what we are and to what we might evolve to.

Time has told us that by breaking away from the routine mode of perceiving of realities around us, we are able to arrive at a new form of original and unique veracities. Therefore, by the virtue of this transformation the human were able to move from tree tops to space station in orbit and someday colonizing the space.

The fact that our genetic design has naturally equipped us to create new ideas, concepts, systems, and perceptions is indisputable. Omar Khayyam, a Persian mathematician, astronomer, poet and philosopher, reminds us of this innate capability in his unique way that

"By the virtue of this solitary, human instinct
The greatest pleasure in this world is navigating in the ocean of
creativity, crossing among the dimensions of realities

People have been considering the origin of creative thoughts as coming from different sources. Early scholars such as Plato and Aristotle, contemplated how creative ideas came about (Murray, 1989). It was purposed that creative ideas were the gift from the gods, Muses, the daughter of Zeus. This idea introduces the notion of idea of inspiration which had direct correlation with madness (Weisberg, 2006). For example, Plato's explanation of a poet's creative product comes from out side the poet's mind. In contrast, Aristotle thought that mental illness plays a vital role in creativity. In recent history the supernatural properties of creativity moved to internal process with fundamental concept (Khatena, 1984). The example of such process are unconscious thinking (Freud, 1930), intuitive leaps of insight, incubation and illumination (Wallas, 1926), and divergent thinking (Guilford, 1967).

A fresh look at intuition and incorporation of sudden hunches brought a new avenue in explaining creativity as a product, a Gestalt approach through the idea of *leap of insight*. The notion of leap of insight in creativity was introduced by Wertheimer (1982) where the creative individual uses productive thinking to advance the previous efforts. In this effort problem can be solved creatively through insight which is characterized by sudden intuition, impasse (a period of no progress), and results in new way of approaching (restructuring) the problem (Ohlsson, 1992; Simon, 1986: Weisberg, 1995).

Besides the influence of insight theory, another movement set groundwork for measuring the psychological characteristic of creativity. As a result a great revolution in psychometric approach to creativity emerged. A group of psychologists developed several tests to investigate creative thinking and creative behaving. These psychologists include Khatena, Torrance, Cunningham, Wallach, Kogan and many more.

The psychometric perspective led to the development of the confluence model of creativity (Weisberg, 2006), which creative products emerges when several factors come together. These factors are possession of particular thinking style that sees a problem in a unique fashion beyond the ordinary way; knowledge base can generate additional information, and personality that allows one to think independently (Amabile, 1996, Simonton, 199, Sternberg & Lubart, 1995). It is obvious that considering these previous scientific works, the role of environment becomes more crucial than ever.

Through the light of creativity and original thinking, the creative and gifted individuals have been able to determine more than anybody, the destiny of the human race. These discerning human beings were not just born because of a pre-destined excellence in thinking and feeling; rather, they grew to this status by being nurtured. This not means only heredity has the solitary role in their excellence, but the great number of research and inquiries testifies to the importance of environmental interventions (Clark, 1981).

When Piaget was conducting a study on gifted children's abilities to learn the advanced logical and mathematical concepts, one of his subjects caught his interest. This student graduated from the high school by age 10 and received a Ph. D. at 18. Piaget asked that student's teacher, how she went about to teaching this child, and she replied, "I water him and he grow" (Piaget, 1978). To enhance the understanding of creativity and the role of early educational intervention; we need to explore some early on contributors and their thinking stances.

Challenges of Understanding Creativity

For centuries people have searched for ways to improve their creative abilities. But, their search had faced with the impenetrable ancient reality that this ability had been ear marked for limited number of individuals who had certain innate capabilities based on their physiological, psychological, or other pre determined compositions. Today, the expanding knowledge of educational interventions and techniques created an atmosphere of hope. These secluded skills and innate capabilities can be learned and practically everyone is trainable. Today's educational machinery can provide means to train human from the womb to the tomb. Becoming creative and strengthen the skills in thinking, problem solving, and functioning joyfully are not only ear marked for few.

Eloquent the multifaceted usage of such a gift, still the small portion of people has performed amazing creative achievements. Still the fact remains, the same that a great portion of population's gift of creativity has been wasted due to poor nurturing and lack of understanding of such a gift. Consequently, barely a small portion of people have embraced themselves with celebrity, prosperity, and self-actualization. With today's availability of advanced information in creativity, it is logical and probable to assume that *the genie is out of bottle* and every one can tap in to this innate capability via early and well-calculated interventions.

Conventionally, the human challenge of progress and advancement in all phases of our history of civilization has rested on the shoulder of few creative individuals. These transcendent thinkers or contributors to human civilization who came from all corners of the globe, whether American, African, Australian, Asian, European, Native American or even those, who had been lost between the pages of time, their progress have always depended on the pedestal of creativity. This unique human resource that constitutes the ability to think and imagine for unlocking the mysteries within ourselves and the cosmos around us is simply not a complex notion, but still yields the most crucial challenge.

Furthermore, challenges in the exploration of creativity are the decisive balance between cognition and emotion and its interactive intensity, regarding to the value formation and morality. Where, the expanded awareness of creative and gifted individuals and lingering drive for emotional depth creates a specific value system in them (Silverman, 2000). The challenge of such nurturing by direct intervention of parents and educators, and counselors should be independent from the idea of a baby's limited mental capability. Additionally, this challenge should welcome and more so value cross-culture's sensitivity and global perceptiveness. The fact of the matter is that the hastened advancement of science and technology has led us to a deeper appreciation and a quest for better understanding of creativity and accordingly availability of techniques to nurture such capabilities.

A further challenge lies in our survival instinct. Like other species, we have been utilizing our abilities to survive and prosper. Some species on this plant strive to survive and grow in accordance with their strongest capabilities such as speed, camouflage, or other means of endurance. For humans, the utmost capability has been the mental abilities. This built-in mechanism is not profoundly relied on the ability to reason or learn only, rather is uniquely endowed with superior capacity of our core universal component known as creativity and imagination.

Faced with these challenges, as a citizen of this universe, come a fundamental responsibility. This responsibility embedded in one of our supreme objectives that we are designed to "create a better life for one and a better world for all". This particular challenge is largely by the virtue of this unique creative capability obligates us to master the art of survival as a species in this harsh universe. As a parent, educator, or counselor who nurtures and values the intellectual, emotional, and spiritual development of a child; you have a great responsibility to face these challenges with utmost willingness, effectiveness, and enthusiasm. As a nurturer of the younger children, sometimes we are faced with three deep-seated questions: *Who* are we? *Where* are we going? And *why* do we exist.

If we try to answer these questions in a global sense and respect the life of all humans, the response becomes more meaningful. In essence the value of being a human makes more sense if we all consider ourselves as a part of a greater entity in a creative fashion.

"Who am I?" can be answered in many facets; a creature with intellect, emotion, ability to communicate and the possessor of many complicated functions. Or, simply another carbon-based creature who consumes oxygen, eat sleeps, thinks, and die What is so interesting is, no matter how we labeled ourselves, the fact remains the same that we are a *physical & spiritual being,* living in one entity, a creature of intellect and faith. *"Where am I going?"* is centered on many directions. Better life, more advanced goals for me, many other ambitions; and finally the ultimate truth, death. In reality, *where* we go is our choice, but the supreme objective of our existence dictates the reverence and honoring the welfare of all mankind, rather than a simple choice of impulse gratification or even a well contemplated injustice. To attain such a noble goal requires a vehicle which transforms us from a *human* to a *human becoming.* The only vehicle can help us to attain such a goal is creativity. *"Why do we exist?"* is a question which each one of us answers differently.

But, if we consider the welfare of all of us, the portrait becomes more focused and universal. To face this challenge, for parents, educators and counselors; sympathetically understanding the concept of intelligence, creativity, creative imagination, imagination imagery, creative imagination imagery, types of imagination imagery, stimulating imagination imagery, and giftedness should be discussed. Human beings have progressed from the cave to the moon only for two reasons; creativity and self-determination.

Concept of intelligence

Intelligence as an innate ability to solve daily life problems and deal efficiently with the environment has been the corner stone of many thinkers. In early understanding of intelligence, the way of interacting with surrounding for the sake of survival and progress became a valid criterion. Nevertheless, defining such a complex concept throughout the history has been an enormous challenge. For years, intelligence and creativity has been used in close relation with each other, as one concept. The early understanding of thinking process, memory, and creativity were all clustered together as one general capacity. As a result of this view the road to deeper understanding of intelligence and creativity was paved.

The early understanding of intelligence was known as fixed intelligence. This view originated in superstitious and local beliefs. Intelligence was attributed to various credulous powers, coming from gods or natural sources. As man understands about his/her environment evolved, so did the view of intelligence in regard to the actual nature and configuration of intelligence. Charles Darwin was the first to provoke the interest of scientific community to the notion of intelligence, as he begun to investigate the *origin of the species*. He proposed the idea of adaptation and growth of the brain and its relationship with the survival of the organism. Following him, Francis Galton in 1869, brought up the issue of heritability in relationship to intelligence and gave an early indication that a fixed view of intelligence, excluding the role of environmental effects, is the way to study the human intelligence.

Later on, in 1905 in France, Alfred Binet showed his opposition to the idea of fixed intelligence and scheme of essential activities of intelligence gain popularity. Along Binet's line of thinking a new and fresh look at properties of intelligence started to come to the surface. For example, Binet and Terman in 1916 characterized intelligence as:

"The tendency to take and maintain a defiant direction; the capability to make adaptations for the purpose of attaining a desirable end and the power of auto criticism".

Additionally, Binet and Simon brought up the similar count that judgment as a good sense, practical sense, initiative, ability to comprehend well as essential activities of intelligence (Sattler, 1988). The debate of hereditary and environmental influences has been around for the past several centuries. Along with, the essential role of each position has been dividing many researchers. Some believed in the importance of the hereditary and others persist on the significance of environment. In the middle of 20th century a fresh look at the combination of hereditary and environment emerged. Arnold Gesell in his work introduced the concept of *maturation and learning* where maturation controls by the hereditary and learning by the environment. This series of investigation opened up the frontier for programming and curriculum writing in the field related to intellectual capabilities and cognition.

During the same time frame, the middle of 20th century, the work of Montessori yelled the fact that intelligence can be educated and thought. A further contribution to the field of intelligence was introduced by a Russian scientist Vygotsky. He suggested that the development of intelligence is directly related to the effects of cultural context on human cognition. Where, the development of cognition becomes reliant on the language progress (Seifert & Hoffnung, 2000).

In the 1970's several important figures such as Das and Humphrey expanded the knowledge of cognition, particularly intelligence. Das, in 1973 emphasized on the importance of the ability to plan and Humphrey in 1979 stressed on the role of memory, conceptual skills in abstract thinking. These days, perhaps one of the most popular definitions of intelligence was purposed by Wechsler in 1958. He defined intelligence as the potential to act purposefully, think rationally, and deal effectively with the environment (Sattler, 2004). By expanding our knowledge in intelligence, another important faculty of human cognition gained the ground.

It was the discovery of the Structure of Intellect by J.P. Guilford in 1967 that a three dimensional idea of intellect was emerged.

In Guilford's line of thinking, intelligence in regard to problem solving has two major properties, the property of divergent thinking and property of convergent thinking. In divergent thinking, the problem can be solved through multiple ways and in convergent thinking there is always one answer of any given problem. With introduction of convergent thinking a new window to creativity, another faculty of cognition, opened up. Though the Guilford's model was an attempt to introduce the notion of human intellect, but more discoveries resulted from this model. This replica consists of three dimensions *content, product,* and *operation.* Content refers to the kinds of information. Product refers to the ways or forms of information received by the brain.

Operation submits the way the brain incorporate information.

The dimension of content elucidate the *kinds* of information reaches the brain. Information comes to human in four kinds. They are figural, semantics, symbolic, and behavioral.

The dimension of product refers to the *form* of information, the ways information reaches the brain in the form of unit, class, relation, system, implication, and transformation. The dimension of product refers to the out come or the faith of the. These ways are cognition, memory, convergent thinking, divergent thinking, and evaluation.

Additionally, this three dimensional model of intellect introduces the notion of transformation which has a lot of utility in the understanding and formation of creativity. Furthermore, during 1980s Gardner raised the idea that human intelligence is set of skills of problem solving which leads to effective product. This line of thinking put the notion of problem solving in new light.

Overall, by looking at the intelligence as the concept of individual differences, three distinctive approaches can explain the development of intelligence as we navigate through these theories (Bee & Boyd,

2009). First approach is defining intelligence as a mean to differentiate people based on their intellectual skills, their ability to remember, solve problem in respect with time and speed, pool of vocabulary and analytical function. This approach differentiates individuals based on *intellectual power*.

The second approach is based on the study of cognitive development in respect with the actual development of the structure of cognition. In this approach the aim is to contrast the individuals based on the blueprint of development rather than the power of intelligence. This approach is called *cognitive structure*. The third approach emphases on the understanding of fundamental process, which makes up the entire cognitive activities. The building blocks, the underlying elements should be taken to account when we contrast the individual differences in regard to structural components and the speed of mental operation, (Bee & Boyd, 2009). This process is called *information processing*.

Creativity

It is a challenging conviction when creativity is portrayed as a mystical trend (Sternberg & Lubart, 1996) or a scientific and measurable phenomenon (Clark, 2007, Guilford, 1977, Khatena, 1978, & Torrance, 1962). Based on the views of educators, a number of them claim that creativity and novelty are highly related and yet it belongs to specific groups of individuals. Yet, others argue that creativity is the ability that we all poses and the creative product can be produced by any one with respect to novelty for person versus novelty for world (Weisberg, 1986, 1993). More interestingly, some psychologists claim that intelligent and creativity has a strong correlation with each others. In some scientific literatures the notion of creativity has been portrayed as the intellectual phenomenon. For instance, Sternberg's theory of successful intelligence (Sternberg, 1997b) expresses the opinion that creativity is one of the three components of successful intelligence. This expression of creativity is allocated by the ability to produce work that is original and unexpected, high in quality and appropriate for its purpose (Sternberg, Kaufman, & Pretz, 2002). Some believed that the climate of giftedness was either based on of productivity and accomplishment (Renzulli, 1978) and others consider that only small percentage of people who score highest on the intelligence test (Terman, 1947) are considered gifted and creative. Now, it is obvious that defining the concept of creativity has been the most intriguing challenge from the get go.

Given direction to creativity as a subject of scientific study, goes back to Francis Galton and his work on hereditary genius. For decades, the nature of creativity and giftedness was condensed in to a single term, cognitive functioning. But, most recent research in the physiology of brain and the function of consciousness opens up a new perspective for defining the creativity.

Until the 1950's creativity tended to focus on philosophical speculation and anecdotal reports (Khatena, 1978), but with the development of Guilford's Structure of Intellect (SOI) model (1967), creative abilities, namely *fluency* (number of responses produced to a given stimulus), *flexibility* (shifts in thinking from one category of thought to another), *elaboration* (adding of details to the basic idea or thought expressed), and *originality* (remoteness of association, novelty, and statistically infrequency of response to stimuli) were introduced. According to the structure of intellect model, creativity is defined as divergent thinking, redefinition, and transformation abilities (Guilford, 1977). Torrance (1962) has defined creativity as:

> *"Process of seeing gaps or distributing missing elements, forming hypotheses, communicating the results, and possibly modifying and retesting theses hypotheses".*
> *(P. 16)*

In 1976, Arieti introduced the concept of creativity as an energetic developmental process of exchange by two open systems, the individual and society. Others constructed test and define creativity in the term of originality (Khatena, 1973). One of the most advanced approaches to defining creativity in a scientific mode was an attempted by Khatena & Torrance in 1973. They define creativity as:

> *"The power of imagination to break away from perceptual set so as to restructure new ideas, thoughts and feelings into novel and associative bonds". (P. 37).*

Another milestone in understanding of creativity came when Clark looked at the function of thinking, feeling, sensing, and intuition (Jung, 1964) and came up with idea that educational utility of the synthesis and integration of these functions is crucially important in releasing creativity (Clark, 2007)

A number of researchers look deeper in the brain and found that each hemisphere of the brain has a separated role in human functioning. These researchers have found some strong links between hemispheric functioning and creativity. The crucial role of human right brain in expression of creativity opened up the new area in hemispheric functioning with respect to relaxation and production of original verbal imagery as a device for creative expression and its utility in accelerating the production of creative thoughts (Yazdani, 1984). Gowan (1978) considers the role of right brain hemisphere imagery as a vehicle through which incubation produces creativity. It is imperative to know that at birth it has been estimated (Teyler, 1977) that 100-200 billion brain cells are already formed in a new born human. Each of these brain cells is ready to learn and function in higher level of expansion. Astonishing as this net work of brain cells are, Sagan in 1977 announced that we only use 5% of our brain capacity through the life time. Though we have discussed several theories of creativity, the greatest impact of this ability can not be understood without further findings about brain functioning.

Creative Imagination

Khatena (1982) asserts that creative imagination imagery is the language of discovery. Definitions of imagination differ greatly, but most seem to emphasize the importance of energy, imagery, and novelty. In Webster (1962), imagination is defined as:

> *"The act or power of creating mental images of what has never been actually experienced; creative power"*
> *(P. 705)*

Khatena defined the function of imagination, 1982 as:

"The chemistry of mental processing where interactive intellectual and emotive forces participate in stimulating, energizing, and propagating the creative act" (P. 107)

The creative imagination was also explained in physiological terms. John Eccles (1972) describes creative imagination as brain activity involving many neurons with a wealth of synoptic patterns, which permit these neurons to form and maintain numerous memory patterns. The exhibition of creative imagination was also mentioned in Eccles work as the exhibition of creative imagination as brain activity requires a unique capacity for unresting activity that continually combines and recombines. He also speculates on the function of imagination and creativity based on secure evidence concerning the way information is conveyed to the cortex with a specificity that makes subsequent interpretation possible. He explained the characteristic of creative brain exhibiting creative imagination as:

"The creative brain must first of all possess an adequate number of neurons, having a wealth of synoptic connection between them. It must have, as it were, the structured basis for immense range of a pattern of activity. The synopses of the brain should also have a sensitive tendency to increase their function with usage, so that they may readily form and maintain memory patterns. Such a brain will accumulate an immense wealth of anagrams of highly specific character. In addition this brain possesses a peculiar potency for unresting activity, weaving the spatio-temporal patterns of its anagrams in continually novel and interacting forms. the stage is set for the deliverance of a "brain child" that is sired, as we say by creative imagination. (P. 40).

Therefore, it is clear that creative imagination is one of the preliminary steps in the formation of creative imagination imagery.

Imagination Imagery

The term imagination imagery has been explained as the form of involuntarily constructed images introduced because of their novelty, vividness of color, and clarity of detail (Richardson, 1969). The crucial role of creative imagination imagery in creative process was highly emphasized by Khatena, (1978 &, 1980).

The imagination imagery as an integrating term refers to those images, which are different from memory imagery. In memory imagery, personal references are involved, such as recalling a scene has been observed previously. With regard to differentiation between memory images and imagination images Richardson (1969) provides a clear example:

> *The memory-image of a hummer that I now have in my mind's eye is of particular claw hammer that is resting on the top shelf of an old bookcase. The visual images of a hummer of no particular weight or type and no other personal reference marks would be a generic Image. But, the mental picture of a hummer with a solid gold head and smooth ivory handle would be an Imagination-Imagery because I had never seen such a hammer until a moment ago when I constructed an image of it. (P.93-94)*

The visual image of that past particular scene, which has the exact physical property of the original object, is memory image. But the elaboration and creation of new physical identity for the object in mind has to do with imagination imagery.

Creative Imagination Imagery

The role of imagery in creative imagination is reported by the testimonies of several creative individuals. Kekule, cited in Koestler, 1964 reported the image of a snake holding its own tail in his dream. This image led him to produce his formula for benzene ring. Einstein, cited in Gheselin, 1952 stated that the mechanism of his thought was not influenced by words or language, but images.

With reference to creative imagination imagery, Khatena (1982) points to the important role that imagery plays in the operation of creative imagination. Gawen, 1978 also relates imagery to creativity based on right hemispheric imagery. Yazdani, 1984 reported that right hemispheric production of creative imagination imagery under the influence of visual and auditory stimulation mixed with calculated interference has significantly enhanced the production original verbal imagery.

Forisha, 1975, studied creativity and imagery. Her results indicated that at lower level of development, imagery is necessary in forming the creative thought. Richardson, 1969 defines mental imagery as:

"Mental imagery refers to: (1) all quasi-sensory or quasi-perceptual experiences of which (2) we are self-consciously aware, and which (3) exist for us in the absence of those stimulus conditions that are known to produce their genuine sensory or perceptual counterparts and which (4) may be expected to have different consequences from their sensory or perceptual counterparts. (P. 2)

With reference to creative imagination imagery, Khatena (1982) points the important role that imagery plays in the operation of creative imagination. Gowan (1978) also relates imagery to creativity based on the capacity of the right hemisphere in production of imagery and he called it *right hemispheric imagery*. Other studies about imagery and creativity demonstrated to the idea of hemispheric role between genders. Forisha (1975) studied creativity and imagery based on both personalities orientation and sex differences revolving around the degree of differentiation and integration within which imagery and creativity may be more integrated.

To understand mental imagery, the distinction between image and percept brings out the similarity and differences between the nature of image and imaging on one hand and the nature of percept and perceiving on the other hand. Image is the direct copy of the actual object, where imagery is the modified and changed replica of the object. In another word image is the same as object but imagery is the abstract perception of the same object.

Types of Imagination Imagery

There are many different types of imagination imagery. In psychopathology some of the imagination imagery is interpreted as hallucination. In physiological psychology, as was pointed out earlier, imagination imagery includes hypnogagic imagery, hypnopompic imagery, perceptual isolation imagery, photopia imagery, and pulse current imagery (Richardson, 1969). For better understanding and classification of the imagination imagery, we are going to discuss some of that imagination imagery as it related to creativity.

Hypnogagic imagery refers to those images that come in the semi dream state while falling asleep. Hypnopompic imagery, images come in the semi dream state while awakening (American Psychiatric Association, 2000). However, Images and metaphors can be explained as a mental processing of information in the non-verbal and the verbal form that occurs by planned activity or freely during the resting or relax stage. Khatena, 1979 explained imagination image:

> *"Imagination imagery activity essential to creative production lies along a continuum of secondary to primary process activation and may be primed and by the procedure discussed to express itself in a unique ways".(P. 23)*

Currently, scientist can manipulate the out-put of original imagery. One report indicates that by enhancing the mechanism of image formation through conveying the imagery stimulation with auditory and visual interferences, the production of imagination imagery reported to be increasing (Yazdani, 1984).

As tools, language and metaphor have been instrumental for convening and expressing the content of imagination imagery. One convenient example is the usage of analogy. In analogical thinking one uses information from a familiar situation, usually stored in memory, with the intention of dealing with new situation that is analogous to the recognizable one(Weisberg, 2006). Analogical thinking can be used in understanding unfamiliar situation, in addition to solving an unfamiliar problem (Holyoak & Thagard, 1995; Klahr & Simon, 1999).

In 1973 Khatena, explained the function of creative imagination, analogy, and images. In his explanation he indicated that the original verbal imagery is a mean of communicating the imagery, while one construct the analogy. Historically, analogy is explained as comparison of similarities between two unlike objects in the context of the listener's familiar experience to facilitate understanding and is classified as personal, direct, symbolic and fantasy analogy (Gordon, 1961).

Stimulating the creative imagination

The function of creative imagination, analogy, and images has been explored by Khatena earlier (1973a). Analogy is explained as comparison of similarities between two unlike objects in the context of listener's familiar experiences to facilitate understanding (Gordon, 1961). The image pattern becomes more sophisticated by adding the categories of simple and complex patterns (Khatena, 1973a). A better understanding of creative imagination and the stimulation of this mental function through environmental enrichment has been a promising prospect. One to five different thinking strategies were used (Khatena, 1982):

1. *Breaking away from the obvious and common place that requires a person deliberately to think in a way that is not habitual or customary with openness for clever, unusual, and novel.*
2. *Transposition that requires the transference of an existing structural or functional relationship of a phenomenon from one mode of expression to another.*
3. *Restructuring, recognizing something that appears to be organized in a certain way in such a manner that it may only slightly resemble the original*
4. *Synthesis in the strategy that requires the creative imagination, to combine bits of information or various objects into something unique.*

5. *Analogy, which involves comparison of similarities between two unlike objects in context of familiar experiences to facilitate understanding.*

Regarding the usage of different thinking strategies and planned environment, Khatena addresses "Developmental acceleration of creative mental functioning through planned environmental enrichment" (1982, P. 121).

Perhaps one of the astonishing findings is the idea of breaking away from considering the cognitive functioning as the most important factor in creativity and giving some weight to the role of emotional domain in formation of creativity. The research has been cognizant of this fact that emotions also play an important role in configuration of creativity. Historically, creativity was viewed from feeling perspective since the middle of 20th century. Maslow (1959) indicated that creativity leaps from personality. Fromm (1995) viewed that creativity is an attitude for living. Clark (2007) stated that many educators such as Hallman, May, Krishnamurti, and others believe that a measure of self-actualization is the criterion for choosing and appraising of creative students. In the recent literatures, the emotional domain has been proven to have essential impacts in formation and manifestation of creativity. Issues such as how children respond to their environment via emotional creativity (Amabile, 1996). Additionally, the role of human emotion on manifestation of creative product, particularly positive affect, has been the subject of some research (Isen & Reeves, 2005). Any way we try to look at creativity, the impact of emotional domain is as important as the role of cognitive domain.

Giftedness

Since 1925 when Terman referred giftedness to 2% individuals who score highest on any intelligent test, many different ideas and opinion surfaced. This statistical break down has its potential limitation. The notion of giftedness as product rather than operation can be explained in its potential matrix. Giftedness based on the excessive expansion of intellectual domain (Clark, 2007) can also explain in a different fashion. The mechanism of *how* to utilize information rather than *what* amount of information should be used as the criterion of giftedness is getting some ground. The strategies of synthesizing the pieces of information and producing it in the form of divergent thinking can be practical. In fact this a good substitute for traditional evaluating process of giftedness rooted in *what* to know rather than *how* to utilize.

Witty (1940) explained that children who are performing remarkably are considered as gifted. With establishment of Public Law 97-35, passed by the Congress of United States of America the definition for gifted became systematized:

> **Gifted and talented children are now referred to as, "children who give evidence of high performance capability in area such intellectual, creative, artistic, leadership capacity, or specific academic fields, and who require services or activities not ordinary provided by the school in order to fully develop such capabilities," (Sec. 582)**

Some of the scientists who explained giftedness in the neurophysiologic sense agreed that the wealth, complexity, and networking of brain neuron are essential in the determination of giftedness (Clark, 1985). By reactivation and early intervention the brain function can improve. Particularly, the earlier the intervention takes place the better result will emerge. The production of an outstanding academic performance, advanced cognitive functioning, mind boggling artistic talent, and exceptional athletics ability are not merely reliant on the genetic pattern. On the contrary, it is also proven to be influenced by the manipulation of the environmental as well. The accelerated development of brain and attitude of caregiver, mothers, educators, and counselors during infancy and early childhood will bring a vast dimension to the growth of the child. If giftedness is characterized as an extra ordinary expansion of thinking domain (Clark, 2007), the early readiness; started at birth will increase the hastening of neurophysiologic development of the brain.

Earlier we discussed the hemispheric role in the manifestation of creativity. In this discussion, the role of each hemisphere of the brain was briefly mentioned. It is a fact that each hemisphere of human brain is capable of different and unique function. The role of hemispheric specialization (Table 2.1) in the tactic of coding and decoding information in human can help enhance the understanding of the giftedness (Wittrock, 1980).

Left Brain	Right Brain
Analytic	Synthetic
Comparative	Holistic
Logical	Imagery
Relational	Intuitive
Technological and scientific	Artistic and humanistic
Breaks down the content	Gathers together the pieces
Digital	Gestalt

Table 2.1: Hemispheric specialization

Gifted children are predominantly advanced in cognitive domain in comparison with average children. Additionally, some of them have some degree of progression in the emotional and the intuitive domains. The way they perceive their surroundings is with utmost interests in understanding the more complex relationships between different realities. These perceptions are directly related to their high drive for understanding and manipulating the knowledge. Their strength and interconnectivity of bi-hemispheric execution of information can aid them to analyze and syntheses in a rate that average mind is incapable of such a speed and flexibility. In fact, their minds are wired to operate in greater speed and flexibility. Counselors, teachers and family members sometimes misunderstand the gratification of the gifted and the creative individuals toward such a need. Consequently, functioning in such a paradigm and gain from this mode of processing the information from their surroundings, sometimes makes them to appear as odd or exorbitance.

As a counselor, educator, parent, or caregiver, it is essential to provide for the gifted child in order to equip her/him for inevitable future. The essence of this book is not rested on the idea of introducing more competitiveness. Rather hosting a child with happy and successful out-look who likes to participate. The evidence suggests that individuals, who made creative contribution in areas of literature, art, and science, are more intelligent than those who have not made such contributions (Ausubel & Sullivan, 1970). Sattler brings up an interesting point that a critical level of intelligence is necessary for creative potentials to be actualized, but beyond this point the relationship between intelligence and creativity is approximately zero (Sattler, 1982).

Chapter Three

GETTING READY

Inspiring creativity in children

Placing the civilization in trustworthy hands of a creative child is the best souvenir one can offer to the world. Several points in educating children, particularly infants have been misconstrued. Points such as readiness, limitation of cognitive capacity, maturation, and neurological gameness has been paralyzing the advancement of human infant and children. To what degree do these points have a merit, when it comes to creativity and giftedness?

First, young children are more capable of learning than what they have been credited for through some scientific literature. Children are developmentally capable of higher level of thinking skills (Edwards & Hiler, 1993), including analysis (breaking down materials to the component), synthesis (putting parts together to form anew entity, and evaluation (judging the value of the outcomes). Additionally, young children can express themselves in a symbolic fashion besides words and language. Furthermore, materialization of imagination is play. Knowing that play is a good avenue to explore the transition between consciousness and unconsciousness, it can clearly lead to creative thoughts and products. Through this active participation between the people who is interacting with the children and the kids themselves, creativity will be inspired. This encouragement facilitates the proper growth of the cognitive and the emotive domains, aimed at expansion of creativity and giftedness, in the most crucial developmental phases, infancy and early childhood. Creativity not only allows the children to be happy and successful, it also permits them to be more appreciative of life. Supported children are happier as they develop the sense of pride about themselves which immediately translates to a healthier cognitive and emotional functioning. However, this act of support is mentally challenging because it requires an enriched atmosphere Figure 3.1.

This enriched atmosphere consisted of four components, facilitator, knowledge, skill, and location. The characteristics of facilitators are vitally essential. The facilitator as a part of enriched environment should be a caring individual with a great ambition to help others to grow. He/she should be a calm, enthusiastic, effective communicator, and patient individual who can manage the time and the efforts. The second component of this enriched environment is knowledge. The availability of the pool of facts, information, and knowledge about the subject of creative and giftedness will provide a reliable source for the facilitator to relay on and help to operate on the practical and scientific pedestal. The third characteristic of this enriched environment is the skill. For utilizing the related activities, the facilitator should gain sufficient skills through programming. By application of the different activities and the procedures in advance and practicing these activities, facilitator can become an important part of this enriched environment. The last component of this enriched environment is the location. Location can be home, classroom, or counselor's office. Enriched locations, where wealth of stimulation can trigger the curiosity. Additionally, the facilitator and knowledge should be flexible. The stance of openness and nontraditional approach to the way of thinking must be the hallmark of this process. These conditions will inevitably create an atmosphere of intellectual prosperity for child and the facilitator as well. By looking at creativity as the ability to generate the opportunities to perceive and use the realities, in new ways, this supportive environment smoothes the progress of persuading the child in seeking solutions within original trends.

Needless to say, the ability to arrive at the novel solutions should be nursed from the first day of life. If in actuality, creativity consists of processes and products; therefore, flexibility and originality becomes the aspiration. Thus, nurturing the basic skills in early age in an enriched environment should be mostly focused on the process and outcome by parents, educators, counselors and the caregiver in utmost spirit of involvement. Assuming by and large, that creative individuals are effortlessly able to generate original ideas; early preparation and discipline becomes vitally important. Initially, providing desirable conditions for the child is greatly hinged on the mind set of facilitator. Following are suggestions for parents, educators, and counselors in preparation for offering a quality standard for raising the creative and gifted child. It is important to place safety first, when it comes to modeling following suggestions:

1. An enriched environment should encourage investigation and exploration.
2. Play with the child with regards to the child's developmental capabilities, and beyond.
3. Incorporate the child's signals and the child's ideas rather than your own.
4. Do not struggle to squash the unusual ideas or ways, but do not lose sight of safety.
5. Consent to child in exploring all the possibilities with respect to originality.
6. Put emphasis on the process rather than product.
7. Use creative questioning and tease their minds without frustrating them.
8. Use a lot of imagination.
9. When you play, accepting that making a mess is a part of creative process.
10. Be positive, encouraging and celebrate each accomplishment.
11. Constantly think of ways to build your child's self-confidence.

Parents who encourage their children's creativity have an opportunity to witness the way their child progresses in a fulfilling and rewarding manner. By jointly experiencing new ways of exploring the world with your child, parents, educators, and counselors foster children's ability to gain more from life and earn a superior preparation for the future. Placing the civilization in the trustworthy hands of a creative child is the best souvenir you can offer to the world.

Becoming creative

In the journey to achieve the creative summit, the climber faces with two fundamental paths. The path leads to the question of envisioning creativity as the product or the process and the path guide to the issue of hereditary versus the environment. The perception of creativity and giftedness has different implication to the different parents. Some parents look at the creativity as a product of cognitive or emotive domains and others perceive it as a process of developmental growth. What ever is your take on creativity, you should envision the idea of *what* is not as important of *how*. Knowing the fact that the process of becoming the creative individual can mature the cognitive and the emotive domains; the early preparation will certainly manufacture a major contribution. This by itself is more effective than the result. The stipulation is that if the *process* is filled with enriched experiences the growth will eventually lead to an effective *result*.

On the contrary, if the focus of training the child is only a result driven one, the possibility of frustration, damaging the interest and harming the gift is highly probable. Because results oriented approach can ignore the incubation of creative thoughts and eventually the joy of "process" will take away the quest for the result. Therefore, the process encourages the *how* approach and result persuade the *what* approach.

Secondly, the role of heredity and environment or predetermination view of creativity versus growth through educational intervention, and engineering of the efforts in the early part of life are contended differently as well. To address these concerns, the focus should be only on the intervention through manipulation of environment for unlocking the creative potentials and accelerating growth as a process rather than final out come with respect to hereditary. In another word, the genetic expression and its contained information are proven to be subject to two phenomenon, *genotype* and *phenotype*.

The genotype refers to the genes that an individual inherits, responsible for influencing the particular characteristic such as eye color. Conversely the phenotype refers to the physical and the behavioral characteristic an individual exhibits through his/her developmental phases and it is considered to be as a result of interaction between genotype and the environmental factors. In a simpler term, the empowerment can influence the hereditary.

The natural course of giftedness and creativity in childhood does not guarantee a wealthy life, ideal contentment, and destine for excellence. But, it brings happiness and success in a sense that can not be predicted and it may contain wealth and ideal happiness. It is the deepening of personality and strengthens the value systems (Silverman, 2000). Piechowki (1989) describe a pathway to enhancing society.

> **The great achievers and the eminent as a rule have a parent or mentor especially devoted to them . . . No doubt it takes considerable dedication and integrity to live for the child but not through the child, to cherish and guide rather to want to own. Thus, the nurturing generation appears to be necessary to achieving ones. The idea behind this view is simply to acknowledge the great importance of those Who nurture the talents of their children. (p.25)**

Thus, becoming creative deepening of personality, stretching the values is as important as developing cognitive and intellectual domains. Therefore, starting this process of becoming creative as early as day one of life becomes vitally essential.

Sutton-Smith, 1973 emphasized the influence of environment during the early part of pregnancy. They noticed that the appropriate environment for fetus depends on the health and welfare of mother. Since the influence of mother's activity on the development of the fetus has been the subject of inquiry in last part of 20th century; issues such as nutrition, exercise, visualization, and some nontraditional modalities have been brought to the attention of developmental psychologists. A mother who is physically and psychologically fit and free from illnesses and distressed, well nourished, and well informed of fetal development has already been ahead of game; she has provided the best possible environment for her fetus simply by knowing and doing.

During pregnancy, fetuses receive their nutrients, stimulation, psychological and neurological supports by means of umbilical cord.

The impact of mother on overall development of the child through this life line becomes extremely important in bearing the child with well developed potentials. Such a preparation, particularly the pattern of biological preparation, will results in having a creative and gifted child.

In recent years, numerous inquiries have indicated that the readiness of early environment, mother womb, during pregnancy has been astronomically credited to the development of healthy unborn child. The core concentration of this fitness has been placed on the neurological development of fetus's brain; starting with the healthy environment of the womb. This healthy environment can attain if the suitable physical health, proper nutrition, psychological comfort, and supportive partnership from father and other possible members of family were provided.

The attempt here is to show the important of successful pregnancy just for the informative purpose. By showing the different developmental stages of the fetus, the gradual growth of the different organs and understanding their functions, a more conducive environment can be provided after the birth. Generally speaking, the fertilized egg takes nine months to grow into a complete fetus, ready to leave the womb at the time of the birth. This incubator is responsible for the growth of the organism, including the brain. Therefore, protected environment of uteruses plays a vital and crucial role in the early development of human and manifestation of creativity and giftedness. The reality is that human fetus lives in this protected and simultaneously vulnerable environment for period of nine months or so. Thus, the biological composition, life style, psychological status, and knowledge of the host have a lot to do with the welfare of the guest!

Before Birth

During the pregnancy a matrix of creation will transfer a single cell to a massive bundle of organs with the identifiable functions and purpose. This period of nine months or so is known as prenatal or *gestation*. During this progressive phase, certain neurological and physical developments take place in three distinct periods; the period of ovum, the period of the embryo, and the period of the fetus. Each period is marked by the completion of certain time frame and the definite developmental segments.

The period of gestation for the human species is approximately 280 days. This period starts from the last menstrual period until the birth. In this epoch the human being goes through three distinct periods the *ovum*, the *embryo*, and the fetus.

On average, about 400 times in the life, woman releases the ovum (egg). The mother is equipped to conceive life in-side of her womb after the successful attachment of egg with the donated sperm of father. When the ovary releases the mature ovum (egg), it arrives at one of the two, *fallopian tubes* in side of mother's womb, where conception can occur. The moving sperm, donated from the father, moves from vagina through uterus and up the fallopian tube, meet the egg and instantly that egg becomes fertilized and life began. This instant fertilization of ovum is called *conception*. The nuclei of this fresh fertilized cell consist of 23 pairs of chromosomes of sperm and 23 pairs of chromosomes of ovum. The 23 pairs of chromosomes from mother's egg and 23 pairs of chromosomes from father's sperm, equally contributes to their offspring's gene structure (Seifert & Hoffnung, 2000). Each 46 pairs of chromosomes, donated by father and mother are made of thousands of genes, compiled of molecules of chemical known as DNA *deoxyribonucleic acid*. After conception, this new fertilized egg goes through the several distinct period of progression known as ovum, embryo and fetus.

The following three sections, the period of ovum, the period of embryo, and the period of fetus, are an overview of developments based on the writings of Seifert & Hoffnung (2000).

I. The period of Ovum

Within the first 24 to 36 hours after conception, the fertilized egg known as *zygote* divided into two separate cells consists of father and mothers genetic codes. This process is called *mitosis*. The movement of fertilized egg begins in the fallopian tube until it reaches the uterus. At this phase the fertilized egg contains up to 32 cells.

During this process, the uterine lining has been prepared and uterine wall have been thicken and flow of blood to the uterus has been increased. At this point the necessary nutrient for fertilized egg was produced by ovum's yolk. From this point on that fertilized egg attached itself to the wall of uterus and the system of feeding changes (Seifert & Hoffnung, 2000).

Up on the arrival at the uterus the zygote cells began to separates itself to two groups. This process is called *Blastocyst,* where *two* kinds of cells form. One, the outer layer, responsible for protecting, defending, and nourishing the arrangements known as *placenta, amniotic sac,* and *umbilical cord*; and one, the inner layer becomes *embryo.*

Two weeks after conception, the ovum is completely embedded and the relation ship with the mother starts.

II. The Period of Embryo

This is a very speedy developmental phase. During this period of six weeks enormous and colossal cells develops; the embryo reaches about one inch and approximately the weight of one-thirtieth of an ounce. By the end of the embryonic phase almost all of the newborn structures, organ, and systems have began to develop. The size of head at the end of eight weeks is about half of body size length. The resemblance to the human can be witnessed by the development of eyes, nose, and mouth. Limbs; arms and legs are essentially bended at the elbow and the knee areas.

At the same time the extension of second layer from the uterine wall to the embryo, is well developed to perform their three decisive functions identified as nutrition, protection, and respiration. Placenta and umbilical cord are responsible for nutrition and respiration, amniotic sac responsible for protection (Seifert & Hoffnung, 2000).

In the mother's womb the embryo is surrounded by the fluid which is entirely filled by the eighth weeks. The task of this fluid is to encounter any forces caused problems by mild physical impact. Moreover, this fluid controls a steady temperature for the developing embryo. Physiological activities such as nourishment, production of bodily waste and growth starts to have a direct association with the out side of the wombs' activities. Since the umbilical cord links to the placenta this connection becomes the gateway to the physical, chemical, and spiritual worlds out side of the womb. The nutrient, oxygen, and a number of other agents in mother's blood transfers through this gateway to the fetus. However, the blood stream of mother and the embryo do not combine. It is astounding to bring up that although the neurons of embryo are not connected to the mother's central nervous system, the emotional stages of mother and mental status of mother during pregnancy may directly and indirectly have some impact on the cognitive and emotive development of the fetus.

Additionally, during this phase, three distinct cell layers begin to develop in a differentiated structures and functions. First layer is known as *Ectoderm,* the outer layer. This layer is responsible for development of sensory cells; skin; and the nervous system, the most important foundation of any cognitive faculties including creativity. The second layer is known as *Mesoderm,* the middle layer, which develops blood, muscles, and excretory system. The last layer, the *Endoderm,* the inner layer, is responsible for emerging lung, digestive system and two major glands namely, thymus and thyroid.

Looking at weekly development of embryo, table3.1 shows the progressive growth based on time and function.

Embryonic Development by week

WEEK	FUNCTION
End of 3rd	Neural tube, the brain forms The spinal cord attaches to the brain Heart is beating The nervous system begins a period of intense development
End of 4th	Head and tail almost touching. Eye appears as a dark circle,

5th & 6th.	Arms and legs appears
	Muscle and skeleton begins to form
	The tail become the lower back bone
	The digestive system, stomach and intestine are developing
	The head grows rapidly and the brain enlarges.
End of 8th	All major organs are present at least in its primal form.
	Some of these organs are functional.
	Liver makes blood cell, kidney removes the wastes, and sex organs are distinguishable.
	The glands have began to secrete
	Embryo has reflexes. Automatic response to touch

Table 3.1 progressive growths in conjunction with time and function
Source: Eisenberg, Murkoff, & Hathaway, 1989

III. The period of Fetus

The last period of gestation is called *fetus*. In the beginning of this phase the first bone cell develops (Seifert & Hoffnung, 2000) and more rapid growth takes place. This period starts about eight weeks of gestation until the time of birth. All major organs of body start to refine and develop during this phase. One of the major developments related to creativity and giftedness, the development of central nervous system, including the brain continues its development. It is interesting to know that the nervous system is only sketched in an eight weeks of gestation. By now the small part of brain and early part of spinal cord have developed. At the third month of pregnancy the massive development of brain and nervous system starts. The continuation of this maturity extends to the first 6 to 12 months after birth. That is why it is so important to start the intervention and enrichment during early pregnancy. This enrichment must be progressive and circumstantial. Due to the sensitivity of each period of the development and its matrix, honoring the enriched atmosphere becomes extremely critical. Table

Nanolla Yazdani, Ph. D.

3.2 shows the development in fetal phase in conjunction with time and function.

Fetal Development by Week

WEEK	FUNCTION
WEEK 12	Sex of fetus can be recognized. Eye led and lips are present. Fingers and toes are present.
WEEK 16	Bones began to develop; ear is fairly completely developed Fetus develop in this period faster than others. Size and length is almost doubled. Fetus heard pumps the blood and fetus reacts to stimulations.
WEEK 20	Fetus is very human-looking at this age; the internal organ lies in a position similar to adult. The skin is fully developed. Fetus has a sleeping and wakening times; at the end of 20th week the fetus is approximately 10 inches long and weights 24 ounces.
WEEK 24	Eyes are completely formed; some fat deposit is formed; sweat glands, taste buds and finger nails are formed;
WEEK 28	Nervous system; blood and breathing systems are developed; the brain is more in control of body, Essential fats in body and brain develops.

WEEK 29-40	Nervous system develops further; Fetus gains about 8 ounce a week. In last two weeks of pregnancy the placenta begins to degenerate and uterus drops lower and body prepares for birth.

Table 3.2 fetal developments in conjunction with time and function
Source: Eisenberg, Murkoff, & Hathaway, 1989

Postnatal development

Beliefs and views about today's new born baby have come a long way from the old school of thinking that a new born baby is neurologically insignificant (Flechsig, 1920) or cognitively confused (James, 1890). Psychologists and the medical authorities are in concord that the babies today are more receptive, perceptive and intoned with world around them than what they have been considered to be in earlier time. Since brain and behavior are engaged in interaction throughout the life span, understanding of adult's brain will help to notice the development of brain during early part of life. Because the structure of brain is already in place at the time of birth, the development during the early part of childhood is characterized as a continuous process.

These early development are composed of building more synoptic connections, trimming unused connections, and myelinating neurons (Poole, Warren, & Nunez, 2007). One of the interesting phenomenons during this early period after birth is known as *brain spurt*. This alleged brain spurt takes place between 6months after fertilization and 18 months postnatal. Interestingly, during this period the brain reaches its peak in number of interconnections between neurons (Nelson et al., 2006). In regard to creativity, a tremendous credit has been given to the first several years of human life, early part of post natal phase for the establishment of originality. This notion of originality (a characteristic of creative thought) develops in the first couple years of human life, is best awaken and rewarded (Sellin & Birch, 1980).In up coming chapters, the principle of postnatal development and early expansion of capabilities of child in the early portion of childhood will be explored on two separated developmental periods, *infancy* and *early childhood*. Each of these two developmental phases will be viewed from three different domains; the *cognitive and linguistic* domain, *psychosocial* domain, and *physical* domain.

At birth child is well equipped with the life. This life which consists of physical and spiritual make ups will be guided to maturation through the manifestation of its blue prints seeded in cognitive, emotive, and physical domains. These frameworks develop and shapes to its fullest potentials through the axis of time and contact. There is no doubt that the old idea so as to a newborn child is an unsophisticated creature who should wait for years to flourish his/her potentials; is out dated and proven other wise. Today's psychologists and medical authorities agree that infants, from birth are capable of perceiving, organizing and learning the information around them in much wider spectrum than it was assumed before. For that reason, the enriched and stimulating environment can and will facilitate this growth and unlocks the child's creative potentials

Characteristic of supporting family

It is important to realize that the role of facilitator in early stage of growth is tremendously vital. At the outset, children themselves are incapable of direct manipulation of their environment and theoretically they have some dependence on the care-giver. In the human species, the notion of dependence on adults can be looked at as an opportunity rather than the limitation. Involvement of family, particularly mother in a supporting mode can make a great deal of differences in child's development. If the facilitation of efforts are seasoned with skills and knowledge, the reliance result become the mean for growth. The followings are the characteristics of supporting families:

- **Receptiveness and involvement:** Be expressively involved and encouraging during the daily activities such as play, routine conversation, reading or any other contacts. The influence of the non-verbal clues is proven to be powerful and constructive. Suitable body language such as smile or loving touch, create a secure bonding between child and caregiver. In addition to fulfilling the security needs, the need for belonging and being loved would be strengthened through either verbal or non-verbal clues.

- **Generating opportunity:** Families should provide opportunities to supply appropriate materials for activities and play. Expensive toys are not as imperative as creative and simple ones! A child may prefer to play in a cardboard box than an expensive toy box because sometimes creativity can be stimulated by the use of imagination in the course of simplicity.

- **Communication:** Talk to the child whether he/she can understand the spoken words. The communication should be rich in content, sentence structure, and descriptive in method of presentation; avoid baby talk. Infants absorb language and symbolic association through visual and auditory channels as early as few hours after birth.

- **Expectation:** There is an old saying that the children perform as well as you expect from them and as poorly as you allow them. Set up you standards high in conduct, communication, and moral representation. Do not lose he sight of safety when striving toward an enriched and well-structure environment. It is a pitiable assumption to think that they are too young to understand.

- **Consistency & Repetition:** According to the Information Processing Theory of intelligence, repetition is necessary for the transformation of information or bits of knowledge from the short-term memory to the long-term memory. This process helps to effectively execute the information progression through the cognitive channel. It is safe to say that consistency creates a pattern which learning become stable. Additionally, repetition strengthens the stability of the learned materials. These two control processes, consistency and repetition increases efficiency and gives support to more fluent and meaningful transformation of information from short-term memory to long-term memory. Therefore, this processing procedure can be beneficial in the development of different domains

- **Challenge:** As a busy adult finding the time to facilitate the demanding needs for growth of the child can be a challenge.

Additionally, operating based on the child's capabilities and limitations can be a frustrating endowment. However, programming the daily efforts with respect to the children's variations of their capacities can make the challenges more manageable and surprisingly, rewarding.

- **Celebration & recognition:** Celebrate and recognize any accomplishment of the child. Commemorate on any of meaningful achievement increases the probability of the occurrence of such an achievement. By celebrating these achieved milestones, the child learns the importance of gaining new skills, and increases the self-esteem. It is prudent to realize that failure may occur and sometimes the lesson learned from failure can be as important as success. For that reason, the facilitator should be patient with the failure through understanding and compassionate.

- **Comfort:** Comfort creates safety and security, particularly at an early age. Sometimes the caregiver feels that the child has been exposed to much stimulation and that may overwhelm that child. This may be very true, but it is wise to look at the situation and see the other possibilities that the fear of over stimulation is unnecessary. However, do not lose the sight of safety and comfort. Actually it is sensible to center the activities on the child's responses. If the child feels uncomfortable, simply stop the process momentarily. Sometimes the discovery mode can become the correct approach.

Child Development

Describing the child's development is probably one of the hardest tasks. Because many different influences affect the layouts of the growth pattern which can be a mean for predication of the different mile-stones. These influences are, nature versus nurture or hereditary versus environment arguments which have been creating difficulties to arrive at a comprehensive theory for child development. However, the fact remains the same that child development is a process which centers around a biological blue print and environmental influences through educating the organism and nurturing different capacities.

For the purpose of this book we will explore the period of infancy and early childhood from three different domains: physical, cognitive, and psychosocial. In the cognitive domain, a great emphasis will be placed on intellectual and linguistic development. In physical domain the role of perception, sensory development and physical growth will be discussed. In the psychosocial domain the concept of self, principle of socialization and human interaction will help us to understand the universal trends of growth for human species and its role in creative behaving and functioning. The interaction of these three domains and their association with fostering creativity will be the core subject of discussion.

Physical Domain

The Physical domain refers to the long-term continuity and changes associated with growth, motor skills and sensory perception (Seifert & Hoffnung, 2000).Changes in shape and size, body mechanics, and locomotion will be the target of our discussion. The most signs of physical growth are changes in the overall seize of body. The other change is the way body accumulates movement, where the movement translate to usage of body mechanism. Understanding of how the human uses his/her body is essential to the early development of creativity. Since in each phase of development, our physical structure is cause to undergo growth, the utilization of our body mechanics goes under the progressive disclosure. That means that each locomotive skill becomes the stepping stone for further development. In this domain we discuss the growth of body with respect to the reflexes, gross and fine motor movements. This will help the facilitator to have an in depth knowledge of physical development of human body.

Another physical aspect is the changes in body proportions. As the child's overall size increases, parts of body grow at different rates (Berk, 2006). In primitive embryonic phase the human configuration is a disk shape organ and lower part, where the disk is head. For example, after birth the head and the chest grow much more than the rest of the body. Additionally, changes in body fat and muscle are considered as essential part of physical growth. Furthermore, the skeletal growth and changes in size, density, and muscular attachment, and their relationship to fine and gross motor skills are the subject of physical growth.

I. Reflexes

Reflexes are involuntary, unlearned movements that take place in response to an explicit and an unambiguous stimulus. Some of these reflexes such as eye blink and sneezing are designed to protect the human from damaging situations or substances. One of the famous reflexes known as *rooting*, a behavior of turning toward a stroke on the chick, assists babies find a breast for nursing.

Another vital reflex is *sucking*, a powerful and rhythmic behavior activated by any object entering into the mouth. A number of other reflexes are intended for survival purposes such as startle. *Moro reflex*. An infant will startle severely in response to an unexpected loss of support. *Grasping* is another reflex which plays a great role in the development of intellect and creativity. This particular reflex, grasping, plays an important role in the manipulation of the object by hand.

Some reflexes, *swimming*, fade as higher brain centers develop, so their disappearance is a sign that nervous system is developing by and large (Poole, Warren & Nunez, 2007).

II. Gross Motor Skills

The gross motor skills include all kinds of movement which requires the utilization of large muscles. This helps individual get around in the surroundings. These are voluntary movements of the large body parts such as legs, arms, and so on. As the human grow older these voluntary movements become more specialized and skillful. Consequently, the different functions such as crawling, walking, jumping and running begin to emerge. The sequential development of this skill will be discussed in detailed.

III. Fine Motor Skills

The fine motor skills comprise of all kinds of movement which necessitates the deployment of smaller muscles. Nonetheless, these are voluntary movements of smaller muscles of body such as reaching and grasping, writing, playing musical instrument such as piano, or drawing which requires usage of small finger muscles. The development of fine motor skills in hand relates to the cognitive development and artistic talents. Additionally, the fine motor skills in other parts of body contribute to the athletic talents.

Cognitive Domain

Cognitive domain refers to the long-term continuity and changes linked to the thinking and the learning process (Seifert & Hoffnung, 2000). Changes in the patterns of thinking, rationalization, memory, creativity, language, and the functioning of the different perceptual channels such as vision and auditory will be discussed as regards to cognitive functioning. It has been strongly hypothesized that creativity materializes by extra ordinary expansion of cognition, emotion, intuition, sensation (Clark, 2007), spirituality, and others domains that have not been discovered. Since cognition, as well as emotion and creativity are strongly correlated, we first discuss the influence of cognition in this segment and in the next sector we elaborate on the role of emotion in formation of creativity.

Creativity has been the subject of many scientific discussions since the mid part of 20th century. In these studies the cognitive functioning were revised on two levels of perceptual and conceptual. Since the mode of the interaction between perceptual and conceptual levels determines the fluency of creative production, several studies focused on the role of cognitive domain as it relates to thinking, perceiving, memory, learning, and executive orders. These studies open a window to a deeper understanding and evolution of the human cognition with respect to the course of developmental.

How does the infant see objects and pattern? How does this perception change during each developmental phase? How does the infant perceive sounds and learn to form speech and symbolism? What are the interactive roles of vision and hearing in the development of cognition and ultimately creativity? In next several chapters we discover the role of perception as a cognitive process that gives organization and meanings to the sensory information to make it useable in future.

Additionally, the function of this process and its relation to formation and enhancement of creativity will be discussed.

Certain psychologists believe that the right timing is essential in promotion of giftedness and creativity. However, others agree that timing is not as crucial as the first group claimed to be. For instance, the issue of *Readiness* that Piaget's theory advocates has been long modified; a large number of theorists such as Guilford believe that the *unique commingling of specific intellectual abilities* can lead to divergent thinking, the bedrock of giftedness and creativity. There are many theories trying to define cognition in lure of intelligent. Each of these theories explains the nature, the origin, and the dynamics of cognition and intelligence in accordance to certain concepts. But, for the purpose of this book, we narrow our discussion to two concepts, Piaget's theory and Guilford's three dimensional theories.

According to Piaget, to understand the thinking and cognitive development of human, the changes in the *form* and the *structure* of thinking in each phase of life is essential. Piaget 1925-1980 explained that the development of intellectual process is based on the cognitive growth. This growth occurs as intellectual capacities of the individual adapts to the demand of environment. In his view, adaptation to the environment is linked to the way in which humans organize the environment they encounter (Glover, Bruning & Filbeck, 1983). In Piaget's view, there are two basic principles in which human uses to develop his/her cognition, *Adaptation* and *Organization.* Simply, humans adapt with environment and this adaptation leads to organizing a pattern which governs the cognitive functioning and operation of that stage. Infants, without exception, tend to adapt to the environment, though the method of adaptation, which may vary. This adaptation takes place by two modes: *Assimilation* and *Accommodation.*

First through assimilation, the child modifies the new incoming information to fit it within the capability of the existing organism, at that particular developmental phase. Second, through accommodation, the infant modifies the existing information or adapts new structure to understand the old information (Piaget, 1975).

Then again, Guilford (1967) bases his theory of intelligent on the three-dimensional factorial cells. His three-dimensional model can be characterized as a cube which involves three kinds of cognitive ability. Different mental abilities will require different combinations of processes and content and will direct to different products (Neukrug & Fawcett, 2006). This multi factor intelligent structure,provides the scientists with a view of intellect as an integrated model that consist of three dimensions, Content, Product, and operation. For deeper understanding of cognitive domain from three dimensional aspects, we elaborate on this theory once again.

Content refers to the *kind* of information; what we employ to execute our thinking. Information can be *figural* (actual image), *symbolic* (printed word), *semantic* (a grammar rule), or *behavioral* (action). *Product* is the form of information. This dimension deals with the closing stages of our thinking. Product consists of unit, class, relation, system, transformation, and implication (Guilford, 1977). *Unit* is the smallest form of object; for example a pencil. *Class* is a group of units, like a dozen of pencils. *Relation* is a point of covenant between units or classes; like by putting several words together we arrive at a new reality. For example words like doctors, nurses, patients, rooms, operations, buildings, and so on remind us the word hospital. *System* is the combination of several relations which they have one general function but each portion may operates differently. The example for system is human body. The human body consists of many different systems, and each system has its own designated function, the nervous system, the circulatory system, the digestive system and so on. Together, these systems provide life; excluding each has its own function. But to manifest life, all of these systems should work together. *Transformation* is creating a new-fangled reality by manipulating another reality. For instance; by rotating the image of a right angled triangle around itself, one can create a cone shape image. *Implication* refers to predicting a situation based on the cues. For example; when is lightening we expect to hear the thunder. *Operation* is the third dimension of Guilford's structure of intellect. We utilize this process in understanding. Simply operation means, what does brain do with the combinations of forms and kinds of information?

It consists of cognition, memory, divergent thinking, convergent thinking, and evaluation. *Cognition* means recognizing that there is some thing exists out side of brain and our brain can relate to it. *Memory* is the storage capacity of information. *Divergent thinking* is a process of problem solving; where if there is one problem there are several solutions to that particular problem. *Convergent thinking* is another mode of problem solving; where there is only one solution for a problem. And *evaluation* means putting all the facts together and coming up with final assessment of any given reality.

Psychosocial Domain

Psychosocial domain is about the long-term continuity and changes in feelings and emotions as well as interactions with other humans. Emotion is a rapid evaluation of the personal significance of the situation, which prepare us for action (Berk, 2006). This emotional dimension refers to the numerous alteration and changes about human sentiment and feelings, mechanism of need fulfillment, social interactions, concept of self, moral development, and personality formation (Seifert & Huffnung, 2000). In a functionalist perspective, the broad function of emotion is to energize behavior to attain goal (Frijda, 2000). Perhaps the most significant statement ever made about emotion comes from Halle, emotions are central to all our endeavors—cognitive processing, social behavior, and even physical health (2003) For the past several decades, the scientist came to this conclusion that personality of the individual plays a significant role in creativity. According to these views emotion are as important as cognition in production and manifestation of creativity (Weisberg, 2006).

As the human grows the identity of the individual begins to shape. In the construction of identity, person's interaction with others, self evaluation mechanism, and mode of functioning in the group, each become the particles of formation of self. The formation of these particles, collectively known as identity, is clearly subject to the capacity of cognitive domain and the reservoir of expressive and receptive language. Furthermore, as the human began to place the self on the social theater, many advance particles emerges. These new particles establish the foundation of person's personality and the fiber of one's moral structure

In early childhood, the formation of personality and moral structure has a unique characteristic; it is raw but highly moldable. In view of the fact that the emotional development of human is largely occurs based on the interactions with the other people, socialization. Therefore, in early child hood factors such as attachment, temperament, personality formation, and socialization form based on our early childhood experiences.

Chapter Four

PHYSICAL DEVELOPMENT IN INFANCY & TODDLERHOOD

Physical Growth

The span of life from birth to the end of the second year is known as infancy. Basically, physical growth seems to be presided over three principles: cephalocaudal, proximodistal, and mass-to specificity. In cephalocaudal the growth take place from head toward feet. Consequently, if the growth direction is from top to the bottom, the infant gain control of head and neck before gaining control of feet. In proximodistal the development happens from midline (spinal cord) toward extremities. As a result, the control of the arm takes place before the fingers. The mass-to-specificity recounts for muscle development. The large muscle and their functions develop first before the development of smaller muscle (Cunningham, 1993). So, within the first two years of life, the physical development is directional, where starts with from involuntary control to voluntary control

Newborn infants enter the world moderately capable of sensing and responding to their surrounding. They can hear, see, taste, smell, and feel pressure and pain (Craig & Dunn, 2007).After emerging from the birth canal, a newborn infant's skin often looks reddish, independent from his/her race. In the first month, the weight increase consists of fat. After few months the weight gain attributes to muscle and bone.

At birth a typical infant weights around 7 to7 ½ pound and measures about twenty inches or half a meter. In term of shape the babies' proportion changes drastically in first two years of life. At birth the proportion of head to the rest of the body is one to four and at the end of the second year is one-fifth. It is important to realize that general physical appearance of the infant may have some psychological consequences, cultivating attachment, a bound between new-born and caregiver which promote feelings of security (Seifert & Hoffnung, 2000).

With regard to physical development, the notion of motor ability has a great influence in the development of other domains. At birth babies are equipped with many reflexes which most of them are design for survival, breathing, sucking, and swallowing. Some of these reflexes disappear after a while and some become controllable behavior such as swallowing. The interaction of newborn with the world around is based on the process of sensation and perception. This process introduces the energy and the realities from out side world to the brain. The brain uses the symbolic application to make these realities meaningful for its future use in the form of memory.

Growth of Brain

After birth, approximately 100 billions neurons in the brain are in place for interaction with external and internal environments. However, the networking process of the brain is curtailed. This means the brain of neonatal looks very similar to adult with several distinctions. First the infant brain is not as functional as adult. Second the size of newborn child is smaller than adult As the time goes on, the process of networking through principle of sensation and perception begin to mature. At seven months past conception, the baby's brain weights 10% of its final adult weight. After the end of 12th months, first year of life, the weight of infant brain reaches to 75% of its adult weight (Freund et al, 1997). Most of this boost results expansion of new connective fibers between existing neurons and accumulation of fatty sheathing named *myelin*, put out by *glial* cell. In another words the majority of this increase is not due to increase in number of neurons, rather is in the development of a denser brain.

From birth to the end of six months, neural activities are dominated by the *brainstem* and *midbrain*, responsible to regulate breathing, digestion, and broad awareness (Adams &Victor, 1989). Around this period of infancy, in first 12 months, the *cerebral cortex* becomes more active and consequently, the number of connections between the neurons increases. As the cerebral cortex begins to activate the more innate capabilities of its regions, the brain becomes denser. This density or wealth of synoptic connections has been proven to have a positive link with creativity and giftedness. John Eccles describes creative imagination as brain activity involving many neurons with a wealth of synoptic patterns which permit these neurons to form and maintain numerous memory pattern (Yazdani, 1984).

The brain of new born includes many sensory functions. As the brain aged in the first two years of life and the process of myelinization accelerates, the sensory input become more sophisticated. Therefore, appropriate training through sensory input becomes the key to unlocking advanced potentials.

Another contributing factor in early part of life, in regard to the growth of the brain is expansion of glial cells. These cells are very crucial in manifestation of creativity. The improvement in teaching methods and learning procedures influence the expansion of dendrite branching and the role of glial cell become more important. This notion of wealth of branches and the complexity of the network of connections among neurons, and the quality of glial cells contribute to the message transferring between cells (Clark, 2007). Since the rate of glial cell production can increase by the influence of rich environment in early two years of life (Rosenzweig, 1966), then creativity can foster by early intervention in this age bracket. The density of glial cells and rapid growth of neurons in size and connection leads to the *plasticity* or flexibility of the brain, which allows different responses to any given environmental situation (Nelson, 1999).

Therefore, the activity of human brain and the different sensory channels such as vision, auditory, olfactory, taste, and so on can be strengthen and advanced in the first two years of life. This sensory and cognitive advancement is subject to two important concepts: sensation and perception. Sensation is the physical stimulation of sensory organ and perception is mental process of storing, unraveling, interpretation, analyzing and synthesizing of in-coming stimuli from the sensory organs (Feldman, 2007). During the first two years the journey of newborn in pursues of understanding the reality takes several interesting paths. At birth, sensation is highly developed but perception is limited and selective (Crag & Dunn, 2007). Different sensory systems such as eyes, ears, skin, nose, taste buds, and other devices in our body including our brain are ready to receive stimulations. The question is; to what degree these stimulations can make some inclusive sense of their actual characteristic is a challenge for the infant in this journey?

Perceptual Development

To understand perceptual development one should focus on differentiation. Infant actively search for invariant feature (Gibson, 2000). Relatively, all of our sensory organs are operational at birth. To establish the nucleus of interacting with the world around us, infants need to be able to discriminate between different realities with respect to their physical manifestations. As a result a memory unit will be formed. As the brain becomes more sophisticated in later part of the first year and from that point on this process require discrimination between the quality and quantity of relevant and irrelevant realities. A great body of the research has proven that this process can materialize only by the virtue of *attention*. Another group of researchers pointed out that all of the senses are functioning at birth and genetically in place to decode most of the external stimulations into the various neural impulses. But, a large number of scientists believes that the active processing of impulses and interpretation of incoming information from senses are not imperfect. Though a small group of the scientists are lean toward the idea that processing of impulses are imperfect. No matter how you look at it, there is always a room for improvement!

This process of perception starts to develop rapidly and modifies over the first to six months. As the newborn starts to interact with the environment, the lack of clarity and stability of the world around them become increasingly comprehensible. To stabilize this uncertainty, a comprehensive view is necessary. Since babies emerge to prosper in an environment enriched by pleasing sensations (Feldman, 2007), we begin to appreciate the importance of a comprehensive view known as *sentimental development.*

The sentimental development encourages various multi sensory interventions gear toward cross sensory modalities. According to this approach, incorporating different sensory input in a sequential fashion will be advantageous.

The importance of developing potentials in the early part of life has been the subject of interests for many psychologists, the wealth of early on contacts turn out to be valuable. As a result of these exposures to the early stimulation in an inspiring environment increase the clarity and sophistication of human perception. Much of the research with human has endeavored to discover that infants and toddlers are active, perceiving, learning, and information-organizing individuals (Clark, 2007). Therefore, fostering learning and creativity in infancy is based on the quality of attention, degree of attentiveness and ability to discriminate essential details from nonessentials.

Visual Development

Vision is the most sophisticated channel for transferring the information from the out side world to the brain and ultimately to the human consciousness. How well and clearly the vision in human species develops during the period of infancy and toddler hood requires the understanding of the developmental sequences of this particular sense.

At birth, an infant can see properly approximately 8 to 10 inches form its face. The can follow the bright light, can discriminate objects from its background and can show like and dislike of an object with regard to visual pattern in less than two days (Cunningham, 1993). For example babies can recognize the face of mother about one month of age. Colors

The clarity of focus or keenness of perceiving object through our eyes is called *acuity.* Theories suggest that a newborn baby has a poor acuity. A newborn can't see objects that are far away or as clear as we can in the first couple months of life. Generally, the infant's vision is poor in the first month life (Seidel, et al., 1997). This clarity improves, as the infant gets older. The acuity for 4-months-old infant is between 20/ 200 to 20/ 50. Most of the children reach acuity of 20/20 around age 10.

The infants can track the bright light even in the delivery room, as long as the source of light is within eight to ten inches from their face and moves slowly. By age 3 or 4 months, infant can use motion, shape, and spatial positioning to help define the objects in their world (Gwiazda & Birch, 2001). Recognition of certain color such as green and red can be discriminated about fourth day of life. Some research indicates color discrimination starts by age two months (Adams & Courage, 1998) and by age six months their color perception nearly equal to adults (Adams, & Courage, 1998; Teller, 1998).

Though infants are interested in looking at the patterns of moderate complexity (Roskinski, 1977) but, they are selective in what they look at. Infants like to look at human face (Slater et al., 2000). The research shows that in the first six to eight weeks of life, the infant visual attention is focused on *where* the objects are in the environment. Additionally, in the dark the infant looks for the edge of darkness and the light (Sutton-Smith, 1973).

Around the end of 8th week the infant shifts the visual interests from *where* to *what*. Since the brain has developed further during the last eight weeks, the ability of visual sensory has improved as well. This monumental shift echoes the fact that energy of the understanding and perception of the world around the infant shifts from *finding* the object to *identifying* it. All of these milestones changes will be corresponding with the different suggested activities to enhance and enrich these functions for facilitating creativity and giftedness.

One of the crucial skills, aiding the cognitive development is *attentiveness*. This complex intellectual developments start around seventh to eight weeks. The mode of visual activities shifts from *automatic behavior* to an *interest*. In another word, the infant priority shifts from unsystematic search and broad information processing to a systematic and selective way to pick up information. This shift helps the infant to ignore the irrelevant information (Sutton-Smith, 1973). Therefore the development of this particular skill helps the development of related skills to facilitate attentiveness skills.

Visual cues and intellect

By age eight weeks, the infant is ready to learn how to ignore or take notice on the visual stimulations. Among these skills, depth and distance perception prepare the infant to internalize the concept of *near* and *distant*. This is known as Euclidian principle which is the initiation of understanding of one's position in the physical world. With this skill the approximation of objects or the notion of *relationship* starts to emerge. This particular skill helps the build a link between the out side world and the mental imaging, independent from the positioning of that object. In another word, if you show an upturned toy-truck to a child, the child is still capable of perceiving it as a "truck". Intellectually this notion of near and far helps the process of *attentiveness*. There are several perceptual properties mentioned by Helen Bee in 1985 that an infant should acquire, size, shape, and color.

Size constancy is the ability to see the size in its actual perpetration even if it is moving away from you. *Shape constancy* is the ability to recognize the shape of the object from different angle. *Color constancy* is the ability to recognize the colors in spied of changing the amount of light illumination. These constancies jointly create the ability *to predict and guess*. Interestingly enough we can say that the prerequisites for mental prediction and effective guessing are the ability to pay attention.

Auditory Development

Infants can hear at birth, but not as well as adults (Seifert & Hoffnung, 2000). Pure tones such as the sound of single note create less response in contrast to complex sounds of several instruments. Toward the end of infancy, the infant begins to sense the soft sounds. Differentiating the pitches begins around age five months (Sutton & Smith, 1973), but making a distinction between low and high pitches takes much longer.

Given that the fetus has heard the rhythmic sound of mother's heart, any rhythmic sounds after the birth can be instrumental in cognitive and emotive development of the newborn child. In understanding the auditory development of infant, it is important to know that the infant can discriminate auditory, different voices, sooner than visual discrimination, especially in first several days of life (Bee & Boyd, 2009). Similarly, the infant's ability to response differently to very similar sounds is remarkably early. As early as four weeks the infant is able to differentiate between speech sounds like "ga" and "ba". Two syllables sounds can be differentiated as early as ten to twelve weeks (Sutton-Smith, 1973).

A few days old infant can localize sounds even in dark (Clifton, Rochat, Robin, & Berthier, 1994). Among all different sounds in nature, human infants are more attentive to the human voice, particularly their mothers, than any other sounds. The discrimination between sounds is the first basic foundation for language development. Reading to the infant may not be a two ways street in the beginning, but certainly enhances the early language and reading skills development. Some research shows the effect of long versus short exposure to the sound and the amount of increase in the heartbeat of a child. In this group of research the infant showed more interest in the longer sound than a shorter one (Bee & Boyd, 2009). Bee also mentioned familiarity with the frequency; length, rhythm, and the point of the origin are recognizable in early part of life. As the infant grows older, more complex sounds can be further recognizable and by the end of the first year the child can easily differentiate many different sounds. For instance, the infant is capable to discriminate the sound of father, mother, and siblings, toward the end of the first year of life (Sutton-Smith, 1973). With respect to receptive language, interestingly, the infant's understanding of certain spoken words comes way before they can pronounce them.

Consequently, familiarity with the words and association of these words with the pictures or the objects can enhance the reading and language development in the early part of human life.

Development of Taste & Smell

Food molecules come to the papilla, and are recognized by taste receptor molecules on the surface of the taste bud cells and the human identify the taste of the substance in their mouth. Taste is the less researched sense. Taste is detected by the taste buds on the tong and the newborn child reacts differently to all four major tastes, salty, sweet, sour, and bitter (Bee & Boyd, 2009). Even at birth, infant clearly prefer sweet tastes (Seifert & Huffnung, 2000). Infant as young as two weeks old is capable of recognizing of sweet, sour, and bitter tastes (Cowart, 1981). Salt solution usually restrains the sucking behavior in newborn child. At birth the facial expressions divulges that babies can distinguish quite a few basic tastes (Berk, 2006). Similar to adults, newborns relax their facial muscles in response to sweetness, purse their lips when the taste is sour and demonstrate arch like mouth opening when it is bitter (Steiner, 1979).

Smell depends on sensory receptors that respond to airborne chemicals. In humans, these chemo-receptors are located in the *olfactory epithelium* Newborns react to range of smells. They can recognize the smell of their mother's milk or mother's breast as early as one week old (Cernoch & Porter, 1985). Though there is relatively limited research available in olfactory perception, some important information is available (Bee & Boyd, 2009). The relationship between olfactory receptors and Hippocampus has been the subject of inquiry in past several years. The newborn infant has the sense of smell and reacts differently at the presence of different smells; especially sharp versus mild smells (Bee & Boyd, 2009). In most recent years several finding indicated that newborn infants' dual attraction to the scents of their mother and the locating breast to place an appropriate food source and, in the process, begin to differentiate their care giver from others (Berk, 2006).

Since the sense of smell and taste are both driven by the chemical compositions, the reaction of olfactory and taste organs are noticeable to the newborn infant and as the infant grows older, these two senses grow more complex Nevertheless, incorporating multi sensory approach in introducing the infant to any new situations through the stimulation of taste buds and olfactory senses, can be instrumental in the development of cognitive and emotive domains concerning the unlocking of creative potentials.

Motor Development

Perhaps no physical changes are more noticeable than the increasing displays of motor skills that babies inquire during infancy (Feldman, 2007). During infancy the early movements are appeared to be automatic and reflexive. Some of these inborn reflexes disappear shortly after birth and others changes or stays with individuals throughout their life spans. Gradually, some of these reflexes transfer to a purposeful pattern of voluntarily movements. The purpose of these early reflexes is only for adaptation of new organism the gravity and the world, out side of the womb. Table 4.1 shows some basic reflexes of infants.

Selected Basic Reflexes in Infant

Reflex	Age	Description
Babinski Reflex	Disappear by 6th months	Toes turn out-ward when the bottom of the foot stroked
Eye-blink Reflex	permanent	Closing eye for an instant
Grasping reflex	Appears by 6th months	Coiling fingers around small objects
Moro Reflex	Disappearing by 6th months	The arms of infant are pushed out-ward
Rooting Reflex	Disappear by 6th months	Turning of cheek in the direction of touch
Stepping Reflex	Disappear by 2nd months	Movement of legs when held upright as if to step
Startle Reflex	Permanent	In response to sudden noise, the arms fling out, back arches, and fingers spread.
Sucking Reflex	Permanent	Tendency to suck at things that touches the lips

Table 4.1: Some Basic Reflex in infants
Source: Feldman (2007)

Certain behaviors such as crawling, walking, picking up the objects with fingers require the adaptation of body with the gravity force and coordination of central nervous system with human skeleton and muscle tissues. The sequential motor development in human species is rather unique, in comparison with other species. For example, in animals' locomotion and using the muscular skeleton functioning matures in lesser time than human.

Basically, gross motor functioning refers to the utilization of large muscle such as legs and arm; and gross motor functioning submits to the usage small muscle such as fingers. Infants during the first two years of life have gone through many motor developments and each phase of this development contributes to the expansion of infants' skills in dealing with the force of gravity and balancing the body. Viewing the surrounding from different perspectives, contributes to the growth of human cognitive functioning. During crawling phase, an infant sees the surrounding from closer to the ground perspective and when the same infant start to walk straight and observing the environment from up right stand point; a great deal of cognitive shift and growth would be marked. Table 4.2 shows the milestones of motor development

Milestones of Motor Development

Age in Months	Motor development
3.2	Rolling over
3.3	Early grasping of object
5.9	Sitting without support
7.2	Standing while holding on
8.2	Grasping with thumb and finger
11.5	Standing alone well
12.3	Walking well
14.8	Building tower of cubs and putting thing on top of each other
16.0	Placing objects in containers
23.8	Jumping in place
24.0	Going up and down stairs

Table 4.2: Milestones of motor development during infancy and toddler hood.
Source: Feldman (2007)

To enhance the integration of mind and physical body for gaining the mastery over the force of gravity, the child should effectively execute the gross and fine motor skill building blocks, mentioned in table 4.2. The effective distribution of energy and mastery over sensory awareness should be nurtured from the beginning; because healthy mind nests in the health body.

Issues and Activities

Activities through out this section are designed to assist the facilitators to support and to advance the physical and perceptual development of the child. In designing these activities factors of child's age compatibility, facilitator's interests and sustainability have taken to account. These presented activities are in accordance to the age of the infant and toddler, easy to perform, and fun to complete.

One of the greatest psychological utility of these activities is the promotion of healthy and safe attachment. During this social interaction, the facilitator endorses love and acceptance and strengthens the notion of trust. A successful execution of these physical activities helps the child to master the notion of harmonizing and balancing in effective locomotion and usage of gravity and its force in relation to muscular activities, for years to come.

Nevertheless, it is imperative to realize that all of these activities should be carried out in the spirit of tolerant and consistency. However, by accepting this fact that a child has to be able to enjoy the childhood, the idea of fair equilibrium becomes a great redeemer. Therefore, if you see the child is getting uncomfortable or board, during these exercises, simply discontinue for a while and try them on some other time. During these accelerated attempts the facilitator should always be conscientious of two factors, *safety* and *consistency*.

The factor of safety is the most important feature of this training. Since the infant's anatomical structure is very fragile you should be watchful of the amount of force, using to aid the infant. Considering the age and the developmental capabilities of the child, safe atmosphere facilitate the quality and the quantity of learning. Minimizing the emotional and physical obstacles will guarantees the secure the wellbeing of the child and accelerates the long lasting learning. There are three factors are important in the long lasting learning: consistency, repetition, and replication (Feldman, 2007).

Consistency relates to steadiness and reliability of performance. There are times during the first two years of life that creates a good fertile ground for establishing the long lasting learning like time to feed, bath or so on. Since stimulating can be provided during the feeding, bathing, changing, and playing periods; consistency on the presentation of the activities and the methods of delivery becomes crucial in enhancing the skills.

Consistency provides a pattern that presents a stable model for cognitive or emotive mapping. Repetition is referred to the recurrence. This factor provides a repetitive presentation of stimuli to the brain. This process strengthens the different dimensions of the message. In each reiteration brain fills the missing part from previously introduced stimuli. Repetition derives from two principles; *fluency* in transition and *speed* (Feldman, 2007). By following these progressive and developmental activities, the transition from one stage of development to the next will be mastered and leaned skills become more compatible with neurological functioning. This provides fluency in performing the learned skill and more complex skills can emerge sooner than when it was anticipated. Therefore, the speed of progress increasers as the child masters the skill.

The third factor is replication. The repetitions of these activities are designed to stabilize the cognitive framework and facilitate the inception of those particular skills in the long term memory. In a simpler word, modeling is a strong tool in learning and developing the mastery of any skill. Overall, the activities are design to move the child faster than actual speed of development in respect to mastery in cognitive, psycho-social, and physical domains; without harming the growth.

All the activities during infancy and toddlerhood are divided into different age range due to specific characteristics of each age bracket. Maturity and capability of each stage content and structure are respected and carefully analyzed for advanced intervention and sustainability of learned materials.

Newborn

Newborn babies are equipped with necessary sensory organs to communicate with the environment. They usually sleep most of time and move in and out of state of arousal, or level of sleep and wakefulness (Berk, 2006).

Activities to consider

1. Perceptual Development: During this month all the senses are ready to function. Encouraging the systematic interaction with the newborn baby to develop and enrich the sensory and motor function of brain and its related organ is highly vital. In the early part of life, especially in first twelve months the interaction between sensory and motor area of brain and related organs such as sensory channels (vision, hearing, and etc.) in conjunction with the movement of hands and feet become extremely valuable in development of cognitive and emotive domains. Babies' progress takes shape from crawling to walking and whole-hand grasping to thumb-forefinger manipulation. These progresses are necessary to the advancement of cognitive domain and psychosocial development of the newborn.

A. Sensory & Motor. The developmental of motor skills at this phase helps the growth of intellectual functioning. At this age the newborn baby is capable of a number of well-developed reflexes; blinking, sucking, rooting, swallowing, yawning, grasping, brief extension of neck, biceps reflexes, period of sleep and arousal (Adams & Victor, 1989).

Activity I. Place your finger in the palm of newborn baby and encourage the whole-hand grasping reflexes. When you perform this activity, make sure your face stays no further than six inches from the baby's face and the baby performs the grasping without seeing what he/she is doing. It is advantageous if you smile at the newborn while you are performing any activities.

Activity II. Before placing your breast or the bottle in your baby's mouth for feeding; gently tap on the cheek, near the lips, to advance the sucking sensation. Always talk in a soft voice (not a baby talk) and smile on and off during the feeding.

B. Visual. At this age the baby is not capable of seeing further than six inches. Also the visual acuity is very poor. In this month and the next, the visual perception of infant focuses on *where* the object is located rather than *what* the object is. The newborn has a great tendency to focus on the face at this age without perceiving the concept of the depth.

Activity I. Draw four geometrical shapes; square, circle, triangle, and some inkblot shape. Make sure the lining of those shape are thick. Place these geometrical shapes near the baby's changing table or hanging from the crib.

Activity II. The baby's room should be well-lighted and all objects should be shown to the baby from distance not further than six inches from baby's face. The room or some of the objects are preferred to be black-and-white or bright colors. Some parents place too many eye catchers around the newborn; it is practical and more effective if you do not exceed one or two eye-catchers.

C. Hearing. At this age the newborn's ears are completely functional. When you talk to your baby he turns toward the voice because this is not the first time he hears that voice; he was hearing it while he was in the womb.

Activity I. Occasional reading and sometimes singing while you pay attention to the newborn is the beginning of the auditory memory building skills.

Activity II. To increase attention span and basic skills in focusing, place the infant on the bed, on her back and snap your fingers, loud enough that the newborn can hear. Snapping your fingers should take place in front of her eyes, not further than six inches. Then repeat the snapping around her right ear and gradually encourage the infant (consider all the safety precautions for not harming the infant's neck) to turn the head or the arm toward the noise. Some newborns may turn their neck or head toward the sound. At this early age, only try to guide their arms not their heads or necks. Be gentle while you aiding the child and also be mindful of the loudness of the sound. Repeat the same procedure for left ear at least several sessions a day. Each session should be about one minute.

Activity III. Provide simple exercises for enhancing the motor and sensory development for the large muscles. Use this exercise during bathing, changing, or drying the infant. Gently, rub his arms, elbows, wrists, legs, feet, fingers, and toes. Be creative and come up with your own activities conducive to this month. It is effective if you talk to the infant at the same time.

The 2ⁿᵈ and 3ʳᵈ Months

By relating and loving your child, you can strength the intuitive abilities during early age. Intuition is defined as thinking without mind and it can be reinforced if the other sensory modalities are applied. This principle is known as cross-sensory modality. The most suitable period for enhancement of intuitive skills is about the second and the third months. Since language has not yet developed to its complete symbolic form, the nonverbal communication between caregiver and infant can be simply reinforced with a number of responses such as smile or facial expressions. Given that the caregiver can feel the child's need instinctually or, intuitively, the child can begin to develop this ability during these months.

Activities to consider

1. Perceptual Development. During the second and the third months the sense of sight, hearing, smell, and touch are critically in demand of expansion. Motor abilities become more voluntarily and infant can reacts more willingly to the environment, though the majority of movements are still reflectively driven.

A. Motor & Sensory. The infant can lift the chest and hold head erect when held (Eisenberg, Murkoff, & Hathaway, 1989). The baby's hand and leg movements are not as random as they were in first month but still do not have total control and intention (Bee & Boyd, 2009). The purposeful movement can be enhancing by keeping the infant's hands free. By removing some of the barriers like the baby blanket or cover from his hand and leg under control environment, you will allow the infant to move and practice *circular movements*. Hanging the objects that are safe for that age from the bed that he can touch and possibly hold will enhance the intellectual and perceptual motor functions.

Activity I. To increase and strength the fine motor activity, or hand manipulation you need to provide several opportunities:
Grasping maneuver <> Using rattles that easily can be handled by small infant. The infant should be able to grasp the rattle and pass it from one hand to the other (Eisenberg, Murkoff, & Hathaway, 1989).
Holding maneuver <> Using the cradle gym that can be placed across the baby's bed or play pen. The apparatus should be placed high enough that baby's arms can reach it. For the safety reason, make sure that the cradle gym does not touch the baby's face. The infant can reach for them and if there is a device that makes calm and soothing sound, the auditory and motor development of the infant will be enhanced (Eisenberg, Murkoff, & Hathaway, 1989).

Activity II. In a temperature controlled room, take the baby's covering off and let the baby freely move the limbs. Make sure keeping the baby cooped up in different situation for more than what is absolutely necessary will hinder the motor growth and strongly influences intellectual developments.

B. Visual. At the second and third month, after the cortex has developed more fully, the optical emphases changes from *where* to *what*. The infant is looking at the object for not only to locate that object but additionally to find out what is the object. Therefore, the focus in the second and third months is *identifying* when last month was only *finding* it (Sutton-Smith, 1973). This basic visual/ intellectual shift is among the early strategies incorporates to explore the world. At this level there is no symbolic notion to name the objects. The reason for that is lack of skills in linking the different relationships.

For physical/perceptual development during these two months, series of activities will be introduced to link the auditory and visual channels together for enhancement of creativity.

Activity I. In these two months the infants are interested to look at the curves rather than the straight lines (Sutton-Smith, 1973). Make four cards, two blacks and two whites. On two cards with white backgrounds, draw a black circle on one and a black triangle on the other. On other two cards with black backgrounds draw one white circle on the third car and one white triangle on the fourth.

Then, Show card #1 and # 3 to the infant for period of 10 seconds each. After a brief pause (5 seconds), show the card #2 for 10 second and then card # 4 for the same amount of time. This activity increases the figural stimulation of optical perception in respect to perceptual/ cognitive development. Store away these cards, after the third months, because this activity will be repeated at age six and seven month with additional instructions.

C. Auditory. Exposure to the regular talking is very essential from the beginning. During these two months you can explain what you do during bathing and changing the clothes or diaper. It is better to be calm or perhaps expose the baby to the soft music, classical or any soft music during feeding time.

Activity I. Use the actual name of people, animal, plant, and objects around, while you are interacting with the newborn. Make sure to avoid baby talk as much as possible because the right pronunciation in early part is not very essential but it is important. If you choose baby talk, try not to do it all the time.

Activity II. For facilitating the intuitive domain, duplicate the noises that baby makes in front of the baby's face and away from the baby's face within 5 seconds interval.

D. Touch. Exposure to the safe textures will influence the development of baby's early intellectual growth. Since the vocalization is in the early stage of development and a number of vocal sounds may mean several things. The usage of sense of touch can be utilized as the second language. This sense can enhance the intuitive domain by utilizing cross sensory techniques to develop relationship with bodily comforts such as warmth, pressure, and stimulation.

Activity I. Massaging the baby's body with hands and different materials will expose him/her to the different experiences. Try to rub baby's skin with different textures. Soft textures such as velvet, satin or cotton; and relatively rough textures such as woolen sweater can be used with extreme caution. It is important to remember that the baby's skin is fragile and issues of allergy and safety should not be compromised. If the baby feels very uncomfortable stop the exposures. Let your child's hand and body be exposed to soft textures but when it comes exposing him/her to the relatively rough textures you should only expose her/his hands to the rough material, with usage of proper common sense.

The 4ᵗʰ Month

The infant begins to use his first imagery or memory formation of the objects around fourth months. When the infant sees the same object from different angles and heights, instinctually reaches for that object. This principle embraces the basic of ordinary memory and imagery formation. From this month on, the mobility of the neck and head becomes more fluent and infant can visualize the same object from different perspectives. By being empowered and able to move the neck and head more fluently, the infant can independently develop more clues in his/her cognition about that object. This is a giant step in cognitive development. The more the eyesight changes from ground level to a higher position, the more complicated the perception of world becomes.

Additionally, in this month the communication channel becomes more coherent, but still is in intuitive form. The infant starts to inspect her hands. They turn toward the sound and them role over from horizontal to other positions. During this month grasping, sucking, and tonic neck reflexes become subservient to volition (Bee & Boyd, 2009).

Stimulation of infant during this month is best served by preserving the responsive environment. In order for infant to maintain the control over the environment, their needs should be fulfilled with the caring attitude. For example when the baby cries it is safer to pick up the baby rather than let the baby become quiet by him self.

Activities to consider

1. Perceptual Development. During this month the sense of smell is well developed and the infant's receptors in the nose are capable of registering different aromas. Additionally, the cognitive processing is more adjusted to the surrounding. This assists the nucleus of differentiation. The infant is capable of discriminating the voices and the images of familiar people and objects. During this month audio-visual channel are more capable of retaining the stimulation and preserving the auditory and visual memories. This memory formation with the additional geometrical perception of environment from higher ground level will help the development of imagery formation in a totally different perspective. Previously the infant was able to see the objects from the ground level. Now she can raise her upper body, 90 degrees higher than the ground level. This behavior will add more *clues* to the previous pool of information which leads to more connections between pieces of information. This facilitating principle aids and expedites the recalling from long-term memory in a more elaborated fashion. In early developmental phases of creativity, this facilitating principle leads to the formation and also comprehension of the unit of reality and ultimately the classification of objects.

A. Motor & Sensory. As the infant grows, the activation and coordination of small and large muscles become critical. At this age some body movements are purposeful and goal directed. These goals are primarily aimed at the satisfaction of physiological needs. At the same time, cognitively another concept begins to form; the concept of *cause* and *effect*. This conception in its physical sense facilities the relationship between the perception and intellect. The infant at this age has additional information about the learned concept due to incorporating larger motor activities. It is fair to assume that every toy and activity can improve the creativity, but it is important to remember that the infancy should be mixed with fun too. Therefore, the intention of mother should be creating a good time which is fun mixed with enhancement.

1. Visual & Hearing. In this month it is important to connect information from visual to hearing channel and vise versa. Bridging these two sensory channels improves the *information processing* through multi sensory inputs which eventually strengthen the fluency of cognitive processing.

Activity I. Put the infant in a situation where he can see both father and mother. Turn on the tape player with either of his parent's voice. You will see that he turns his head toward the person whose voice was heard through the tape recorder. Repeat this several times a day for three times a week during the fourth month. If the infant was not able to look at the person talking on the tape, pair the sound on the tape with the respected parent's voice. For example, the father has to repeat simultaneously the same sentence on the tape.

Activity II. Find out what kind of sounds you are able to make with your mouth; birds, bells, dog, or so on. There are only four distinctive sounds necessary in this activity. Then provide a picture of four things that for which you are able to make sounds. Show the object or the animal to the infant as you making that particular sound of that object or animal.

Activity III. Place the object in different places and different heights and encourage the infant to reach for it.

Activity IV. Place a toy which rattles and makes noise above the infant's bed, where he/she can hit it. By hitting the toy accidently first, he/she discovers the principle of cause and effect. Later on this behavior becomes purposeful and the child hits the toy for making noise.

For the 5th and the 6th months

In the fifth and the sixth months, the bone structure of the infant is strong enough to support the commencement of sitting, holding the head above the horizon, and arching the back (Einseberg, Murkoff, & Hathaway, 1989). As soon as the infant finishes the sixth month, he/she can hold an object in one hand and directing it to her mouth, without looking at it (Bee & Boyd, 2009). This is one of the key elements in the development of creativity.

Provoking interests in objects is generally dependent on two factors: complexity and curiosity. *Complexity* is defined in the many different ways in which an object can transmit the information. In the human species, the drive for exploratory behavior and curiosity is linked with novelty and diversity of pattern of an early age (Berlyne 1960). Children in this age range show more interest and curiosity toward the more complex objects than simple ones.

Activities to consider

1. Perceptual Development. Through the fifth and the sixth months, the infant learns more complicated strategies to move around. The tonic neck reflex has disappeared and his/her entire limbs are independently can move (Adam & Victor, 1989). He/she can turn one side to the other and sit with the help. Some infants can start to crawl and independently discover the surroundings. The visual perception is fully focused to identify objects and *what* the object is by trying to reach and grasp it (Sutton-Smith, 1973).

A. Motor & Sensory. Given that the hands and legs, each can move separately the right and left hemispheric motor skills are maturing. Additionally, both hand grasping in regard to eye hand coordination and hemispheric specialization can be strengthen at this early age. Knowing that the left hemisphere is designed for the analytical manipulation and the right hemisphere devised for the synthetically formation; the bilateral training of both hemispheres can begin at this junction. In preparation of right hemispheric empowerment, it is crucially necessary to let the infant manipulate things with his/her left hand

Activity I. Provide opportunities for the infant to utilize both hands. Since the transaction of motor and sensory information for the right side of the body come from the left hemisphere and visa versus for left side (except vision which goes to both hemispheres, no matter which eye received the stimulation); the localization of brain activities can be strengthen.

Activity II. On a regular basis, place the bottle or any object of interest in the infant's left hand.

B. Visual. Exploring the environment and the wealth of different visual exposures during these two months is important. Since the eyes are skillful enough to follow the object and search for it in space, the simultaneous stimulation of vision and memory becomes instrumental. Through this stimulation you can strengthen the cognitive domain by teaching the child the notion of *anticipation*. Activities such as exposure to the different parts of the house and out doors are recommended. Additionally, complex patterns provoke curiosity in infants (Berlyne, 1960).

Activity I. Colorful pictures with variable content such as animals, plants, people, landscapes, or geometrical shapes, will develop the vast range of visual perceptions. These presentations should be accompanied with naming the pictures and asking the infant to point at the different pictures.

Activity II. Place your child on her chair and put a toy which can make noise, preferably a solid color, in front of her. Allow her to look at it and listen to the noise that the toy usually makes for 5 or 10. Then place a piece of thick paper, a contrasting color to the toy, between your child and the toy. At this point, the child may look straight at the paper without removing the paper to rediscover the toy. If she did not look for the toy behind the paper, which she usually would not, activate the toy's noise and give her a clue to find the toy behind the paper. Repeat this three times a day. If the child can't find the toy behind the paper after several trials, then remove the paper and let her discover the toy. Then, continue the same process until she gets the idea. After she masters this skill just repeat the activity once a week.

Activity III. Show more complex pictures of many different shapes and configurations to the child. Change this picture several times during these two months. Each time you expose your child to these pictures, make sure the picture is close enough for your infant to see them without straining his/her eyes. Allow the child to learn the name of these pictures and expect the child to name them as he sees them.

Activity IV. Train the child to follow different objects at the same time in space. You can use three toys at the time.

Activity V. Place the object under a cloth and encourage the child to look for it under that cloth. If he/she can't find it or doesn't know how to go about it, try to coach him/her.

B. Auditory. Use auditory channels to increase the vocabulary pool of the infant. This should be combined with movement which explains the learned vocabulary to enhance the *original imagery*. Original imagery is the important foundation for producing creative thinking. Language development can enriched during these months by reading stories to the child.

Activity I. Since motion is more comprehendible by the right hemisphere and recognition of an object is more graspable by left the hemisphere, these two channels can reinforce each other. Putting these two channels of perceiving to work together enhances the development of early formation of creative thinking. Place a toy bird or a picture of a bird in front of the child and after the child observes it for at least 10 seconds, tell the child that it is a bird. Then pick up the toy bird or the picture of the bird and act as if it is flying and tell the child "bird is flying". Move the picture or the toy in the air back and forth, slowly and just say: "flying". You can come up with other toys and related actions. The principle idea is to associate *noun* with the *verb*. You can show bird outside flying and bring it to your child's attention. Repeat this exercise several times. After finishing with this part; pick up the child and hold him safely, up in air. Floating him gently and say: "Flying."

C. Touch. Provide cross-sensory information processing by utilizing three senses, touch, vision, and hearing for deeper cognitive development.

Activity I. Play the touch game with the baby. During bathing or changing, touch the hand, foot, head, ear, nose and so on. When you touch each part make sure you name them at the same time. Allow the child to see your mouth movements. Additionally, reverse the game and hold his hand and touch same parts of your body and name them. Take your time and do not rush; the baby should be able to encompass enough time to digest the information. As a side, avoid genital touching as this undermines the establishment of appropriate boundaries.

From 6th through 12th Months

One of the significant transitions in this period is the development of more complex fine motor skills. Most activities ought to be focused on the effective and polished extension of this motor development. Usage of fingers, hand and thumb increase the coordination of grasping and better conceptualization of the object. This firm support of an object by finger, thumb, and palm procure more time for the brain to perceive and conceptualize. By using play, babies can practice from many different perspectives, the notion of cognition. Playing games such as peek-a-boo, patty-cake or waving bye-bye increases fine motor ability and interaction with adults. This process strengthens the cognitive, psycho-social and physical domains in a cooperative manner. On the other hand the development of gross motor skills advances in this age bracket. Since the gross motor development encourages movement while the child explore the cognitive functioning also progresses. The combination of fine and gross motor development is a period known as *visual guided search* (Rochat, Goubet, & Senders, 1999).

Activities to consider

1. Perceptual Development. In the last six months of the first year, the child shifts from not bearing weight on legs to standing up and taking steps. Self-feeding and manipulation by fingers reaches a new level of control and self-regulation. Vision and hearing become more interactive and builds the final bridge to speech utilization through symbolic behaviors (child can use words and express agreement and

disagreement, by utilizing eyes and ears; e.g. nodding head side to side for disagreement.)

A. Motor. Now the child can start to stand up by holding on to someone or something. Later on she can sit without support and crawl to get a toy out of reach. During these six months she gains mobility through hands-and-knees locomotion and crawling shifts to hand-and-feet posture to pull up to a standing position (Sutton-Smithy, 1973). By the beginning of the tenth month, the child can pull up to a standing position and assisted walking by holding on to furniture for smoother cruising.

Activity I. Since the child's locomotion is varied, the best activity to apply is encouraging the child to stand up, sit down, and walk at various speeds by the aid of a care-giver. Make sure the safety procedures are observed.

Activity II. Encourage the child to move a toy or object from one hand to the other. During this activity the child uses a combination of grasping, placing the object in the mouth and following the object with the eyes.

Activity III. Place a toy piano in front of the child and let her play and bang on the keys. Also, you can introduce simple notes, by playing them and allowing the child to imitate you.

B. Visual. The child should be encouraged to pick up any toys he/she drops. Picking up toys with fingers is important. Throwing a ball and chasing it is encouraged. Manipulation of thumb and forefinger requires a more sophisticated occipital and frontal cortex involvement via eye-hand coordination. At the end of eleventh and the beginning of the twelfth month the child becomes color conscious and starts to identify colors and associate them with language. The ability to associate two objects of the same color becomes a great vehicle for advancement of the cognitive and emotive domains. The eyes are more capable of seeing distance and visual memory can be stored in an expedited fashion.

Activity I. (Age 6, 7, &8 months): During these three months the basic impression of geometry can be mastered. This activity consists of presenting two different sizes of spoons or pieces of paper to the child. Start from the small size to the big size, in sequence and name them "small spoon" and "big spoon". Let the child internalize the different sizes. Each time you show the spoon, bring to the infant's attention the size of the spoon. Show the child the big and small. Then after repeating this several times let the child touch those objects.

Additionally, use the visual activity I for age two and three months (Figures 4.1). This time you show the cards with white circle and black circle together at the same time for a period of 5 seconds. Then, show the child the cards with black and white triangles, simultaneously for five seconds. Then place all of the four cards in front her and let her look at them. During this observation period you should name the shapes and the colors.

[Verbal encouragement and personal attention is vitally important]

Activity II. (Age 6, 7, &8 months) Show the child the pictures of different birds, fish, or any thing from the same class to reinforce the notion of *classification* and also say, "See, they are the same kind." Use this activity with other objects or animals.

[Verbal encouragement and personal attention is vitally important]

Activity III. (Age 9, 10, 11, & 12 months) While the child is sitting, show the child two totally different objects, but the same color, and encourage the child to understand the similarity of colors in the two different objects. Use all the colors in this experiment. When you take strolls or short walks with your child, repeat the colors in nature and try to make her recall the similarities. "What else is green?"

Activity IV. (Age 9, 10, 11, & 12 months) Put several simple objects like a key, spoon, paper, and two more objects in a plate and ask the child to hand you one of them. Make sure that safety factors are observed because the child at this age has a habit of placing things in the mouth. Each time the trial is successful, reward the child with verbal or behavioral praise (thank you or soft pat on the back). Also start to count and associate numbers with quantity of toys. It is very important for the child to learn the mathematical value of (1). This mathematical activity should start from age six months and intensify as child grows older.

Activity V. (Age 9, 10, 11, & 12 months) Ask the child to close his eyes and place a key or another simple object like a coin in his hand, while holding his hand closed. Then ask him to identify the object without opening his eyes. You can place the object under the cloth and ask the child to manipulate it with his hand and tell you what the object might be. Ask the child to give you one and then two of the same objects. When you ask her to hand you two coins; show her two fingers and say, "One and one is two," Then repeat the same principle with coins. Placing one coin next to the other and say, "One and one is two."

2. Language & Auditory Development. Due to the closeness of acquisition of language skills and auditory development, the enhancing activities are combined. During this age of development the child is moving from cooing to babbling. Before the first year finishes, he can even use a two to three-word sentence and has a vocabulary pool of 40 (Sutton-Smith, 1973). This transition from cooing to forming a simple sentence requires a great deal, of attention. What intellectually is happening in this transient stage is the movement of information from audio-visual representation to a symbolic coding and transforming product, *words*. In other words the child has a word for the object and can label it. Therefore, an object represent in the mind in the absence of sensory registration.

This transition is one of the most important events in the life of a creative individual because it takes words to express thoughts. From this point on there is another mental reference to a single reality; there is a word *dog* for an object *dog*, in the child's mind. Manipulation of this transition can strongly influence the wealth and methodology of synthesizing of the different realities; in other words, a solid foundation for the creative mind.

Activity I. Read the children books with pictures and words. Encourage the child to answer simple questions pertaining to those pictures; particularly action and movements. For example, ask:

"Show me the bird?" Additionally try to encourage them to pronounce different words from that story or the book you read to her. Then encourage them to talk about the action by saying, "Tell me what is going on in this picture?"

Activity II. (Age 10, 11, & 12 months) Make or obtain cards with the pictures of different animals and people. Then play an imaginary game with the child by encouraging him to speak. Provoke his curiosity by making the sound of a dog or cat and ask him to pick up the card with the picture of the dog or cat. Then make a simple two to three words sentence and continue the rest of the cards with the same fashion. Make sure when you make your sentences, referring to different animals, use a slightly different combination of words. Avoid baby talk at all times.

Activity III. Have a serious conversation with your child as if she can understand you perfectly. Pause occasionally and look at her and show the expression that you want her opinion or response to your statements. She may not understand all you said but, she will learn the pattern and process of two-way communication. Use the different emotional expressions and body language during you conversation with her. Dinner table with the entire family member gives a great opportunity to expand the language and social skills.

Activity IV. Play games such as the "itsy-bitsy spider" to increase eye hand coordination of movement and vocabulary pool. Verbal encouragement and personal attention is vitally important

From12ᵗʰ through 18ᵗʰ Months

By 12 months most infants are four times heavier than they were at birth. They are able to stand alone during this phase and they are not called infants. At this age, the child is called a *toddler.* The ability to stand up and be mobile and walk around gives totally different perspectives to the physical, cognitive, and psychosocial functioning. They can experience things dependently, they see the world around them from different levels and they feel they can go to the world rather than someone bringing the world to them. Activities in this phase should be monitored carefully due to boldness and lack of experiences from the toddler's side. They are very observant and love to imitate other's physical movements. Curiosity mixed mobility in the absence of rational reasoning regarding dangerous situations can lead to harm easily. As a conscientious facilitator, you should always supervise the toddler closely during this exciting age.

Activities for Physical development

1. Perceptual Development. The physical movement and navigation of the toddler at this particular period starts a long lasting pattern of movement and locomotion that keeps perfecting its function throughout the rest of the life. In the earlier part the child's development, movement was varied from rolling to crawling and finally to walking. Cognitive and emotive development in conjunction with locomotion begins to establish some stable routines. When the child begins to independently move around and have a more control over his movements, a unique position can be created the *concept of self and the concept of the world.* Who am I? And, what is out there begins to emerge in one's identity. In the beginning of the toddler phase, these two concepts of self and the world are not clearly differentiated. As the toddler develops, these two concepts begin to clearly differentiate.

A. Motor. At one year of age, the child can walk with some help. But as she grows older, she can become independent walker. She can climb up the stairs or couch. Also, she can manipulate objects with forefingers and thumb which opens up a new door for concentrating on the object and examining that object from many different angles and positions (Sutton-Smith, 1973). That will help her to expand the detail learning and the concept of *unit*. Examining the object from different distances establishes a conscious base for making different choices.

Activity I. Place a toy seven to eight feet, away from your child and encourage him to go and get the toy. Make sure you put the toy away from him at different angles. Then encourage him to say a few words about it. Example, "tell me what did you do?" "What did you get?"

Activity II. Place the healthy dry food several feet away from your child and ask him to go and get it. After getting it, tell him to bring it to you and then eat the dry food together.

B. Visual. During this age the toddler is more interested in exploring. Place several pairs of different objects with the different shapes and colors at a relatively far distance, twenty feet. These objects could be red and yellow balls; a pair of small balls and another pair of large one. Then select one object at a time based on size and color. Then instruct the child to bring you the ball. For example, "Bring me the big red ball." This activity strengthens the intellectual functioning based on the association of words with visual images of the object. The other vital part of creative thought is the notion of *flexibility*. This skill can be facilitated during the toddlerhood.

Activity I. Try to use pictures of various objects, such as plants, animal pictures, or people in your activity. After showing those pictures, remove the picture and simply refresh the memory of the child by asking the child to go by, touch, bring, and stand next to that picture.

Activity II. This activity teaches *classification*. Place five red and two green wooden or plastic blocks in front of your child in two groups. Then tell the child that one group of blocks is green (point to the green blocks) and the other group of blocks is red (point to the red ones). Then ask the child to give you all the red blocks and you place them together in same configuration in front of you. Repeat the same procedure until the child gives you all the red ones. If she makes a mistake correct her and continue until she becomes fluent in classification. You should repeat the same procedure for green blocks. Each time the child goes through a correct trial reward her.

2. Auditory. Hearing at this age can become a great avenue for the development of cognitive and emotive domains. In view of the fact that the brain is ready to accept bi-lateral input in an analytical and synthetically fashion, relaxation can be utilized. Relaxing through stimulating the right brain can improve the creative thinking ability. To provide relaxation, you have to activate the left hemisphere.

Activity I. This activity creates a relaxed atmosphere and activates right brain functioning. Fifteen minutes before the sleeping time, place the child in his bed and turn on soft music, with no words. Make sure the lights in the sleeping area would not be too bright but the child should be able to see his surroundings.

By listening to the soft music or nature sounds (like rain or crickets), the left brain becomes preoccupied and the right hemisphere generate a relaxing sensation. In this position, the chance of creating visual imagery and fantasy production is highly facilitated.

C. Taste. Developing health dietary habits in the early age can indirectly influence creativity. The healthy body can host much productive imagery. Experiencing a wealthy of tastes helps to establishment sensory enrichment. Since memory recall is stimulated by flavor and smell; the utilization of these two senses can enhance creativity. During this early age, introducing a variety of various stimulations, train the mind to become a flexible agent. This *Flexibility* is one of the four characteristics of creative thinking, Torrance, 1974 (*fluency, flexibility, originality, and elaboration*).

Activity I. Simply, expose your child to a variety of different food. The exploration of different aroma and taste are encouraged. This exposure should be with utmost consideration to the comfort, safety, and health issues.

Second six months of 2nd year

From 18 to 24 months the life of toddler becomes defined in greater detail than was before. They can jump, they can peddle a tricycle, and they can hold the pen and draw. The mastery in locomotion and physical development aids the expansion of cognitive abilities, language capability, and social interactions. This opens a new section in the child's development. Though each child starts to act differently at the different times, during the last half of the second year, the mission of facilitator remains the same, nurturing and consistency with love and room to grow independently.

In this developmental phase the socialization of the toddler is enhanced by *play*. This interactive mechanism of voluntary behavior, play, has gaining increasingly attention during the last few decades (Eizenberg, Murkoff, & Hathaway, 1989). Play can be instrumental in stimulating the cognitive and psychosocial domains, and stretching several drive mechanisms. Drive mechanisms such as curiosity, convergent thinking, and divergent thinking (Guilford, 1962) can accelerate the shift of thinking from sensory responses that the child is accustomed, to more directional thinking which can be characterized as pre-concrete or elementary logical thinking. Parents, who spend time with their child, encourage exploration, play, and use complex language have children who later perform higher in intelligent assessments, (Bee & Boyd, 2009).

Moreover, in these six months, the social development and personality formation of the toddler undergoes a radical change; from instinctual to more differentiated and autonomous means. All of these changes, to some degree, are contributed to the independent capability of mobilization. When the child plays and utilizes physical movement, in this age bracket imagination helps the skill gaining. Perhaps one of the crucial developments in the second part of second year is physical development. The physical movement mixed with imagination and usage of play proves to be instrumental in the development of the other crucial functioning of the toddlers as well. For example, play can contribute to the psychosocial development or membership in the group.

This maturation process most likely takes place in social settings. Success and failure, experienced during play, can greatly influence the concept of self and self-worth of the child.

Interestingly, at this age toddlers have some orientation from the environment in their consciousness. In other words, they can speak and have some symbolic references in their memory from the world around them. While they play, they can make use of the world in their mind with symbolism and language. This communication skill as an arbitrary system of symbols allows them to interact with each other. This transition from cooing and babbling to two-word sentence with capacity of more than 50 words are crucially important in this age bracket (Sutton-Smith, 1973).

The importance of this last six months of the second year of life, is to bridge sensory responding and logical thinking. When thinking shifts from relatively simple sensory responses to more complex logic, the issue of storage of information and transformation of actual reality to fantasy becomes a matter of utmost attention. Here, the sudden shift with the limited channel of communication creates a condition for human intellect *to anticipate,* the early foundation for *predication;* based on memory and complex *relations* between bits of information. In this paradigm the role of *play* becomes extremely essential.

Play

Through the history of human interaction, whether it was governed by myths or science, the notion of play and human growth has been documented. In some early documentation approximately 5000 years old, in China, a selective group of newborns were separated from their parents and exposed to series of training or play. Consequently, finishing the series of training would help to choose the designated person for becoming the rulers of the future China. In the historic search we see plenty of documentation that plays has served a crucial role in the development of children. Play varies in different cultures. But most play of toddler-hood and early childhood is designed for developmental purposes. Each culture is full of different kinds of play.

In modern times the value of play has been tremendously discussed in the formation of intellect, social and cultural development, (Eizenberg, Murkoff, & Hathaway, 1989). Even some sophisticated play is designed for motor and sensory development has been used in the treatment and the rehabilitation of geriatric individuals or patients with neurological conditions. Over all, play has been used as long as human could utilize his/her imagination. In ancient times play was mostly used in an esthetical sense, for amusement, social interaction, and child development.

Play as a function has no formalized definition. The fact is that play has been with humans and animals from the beginning and the significance of that can't be ignored. Some biologists strongly believe that in the animal world, play is considered as academic circles to teach the instinctual skill building for the maturation of mechanisms for basic needs fulfillment. Equally important, most anthropologists agree that play has been used in primitive cultures and moderns as well, for the same reasons. Therefore, play as a teaching tool assists the transferring information, tradition, history, health virtues, and culture as a whole. Bruner (1968) considered play, voluntary behavior, which has five characteristics, anticipation of the goal and means of reaching that goal, freedom from immediate sensory control, ability to maintain beyond a single response, the situational ordering of response, and voluntary behavior that demands skill. There are several issues which are important in *play*; curiosity, cognition, and creativity (Bruner, 1968).

Curiosity and Play

In children age 18-24 months, the concept of curiosity plays a role as a *drive* for exploratory function. The human brain as an entity which is constantly preoccupied with interaction with the internal and external world has an *exploratory drive*. This drive may emerge from arousal of mixed and conflicting responses (Berlyne 1960), in which that conflict may lead to novelty as a psychological, rather than simple physical qualities. For example, take the case of a child holding a fur, toy bear. This bear, if pushed by the ear, is capable of growling and this noise frightens a child. The comfortable toy with out pushing its ear creates a *compatible* response for the child. But when its ear was pushed, the loud noise becomes *incompatible* response in the child mind and those clashes in his cognition. To reduce this conflict, the child explores the novel object, which produces the exploratory response, and the child learns to hold the bear with out pushing its ear (Bruner, 1968).

Therefore, during the activities that require some degree of freedom given to the child to explore the reality and enhance his/her curiosity, freedom of the choice must be respected. In other words let the child learn and acquire trust.

Cognition and Play

Play is considered actual cognitive function. Either we use a series of verbal, physical, or other means in a systematic fashion or imaginative compensations; the mental operation is in progress (Bruner, 1968). This active intellectual function being performed based on situational understanding and modeling. In two year olds, cognition shifts from *discovery* to *invention*. Therefore, the idea of play as a cognitive behavior becomes more selective and formative. Selectivity is assumed to be a vehicle for aiding the child to operate independently from the trust on caregiver to independency or autonomy. This cognitive jump is a part of a healthy process of development and growth that it may be hard for some mothers to let go. Through playing, this crucial separation from mother's attachment helps the toddler to claim independency.

In all play activities, the preoccupation of the toddler to some portion of play must be honored. Let the child play the way he/she wants to play. Consideration should be given to the safety; the child should be free from over instructions.

Creativity and Play

Most of the play has been compromised based on many different individual and environmental circumstances. The only remedy in these situations has been our imagination and creativity. Research strongly suggests that children, who use their imagination in playing, score higher in creativity tests (Bruner, 1968). Playing imaginatively helps the socialization and novelty of toddlers. Involving the children from an early age in playing can improve several imperative functions namely, physical and motor development, emotional and affective expressions, sense of humor, and most of all flexibility, originality and fluency, (Torrance, 1962). Play is a great opportunity to incorporate all of these characteristics in to thinking blocks.

There will be several suggestive ground rules for any playing activities. These ground rules enlighten your knowledge and facilitate your skill in designing and executing a fun, enriched, and creative provoking modalities. One of the important forms of information arrangement skill which the child is ready to master between 18th to

24th months is the notion of *relation*. By now the child has mastered units of information, class, and now he/she can learn *relationship*. The affiliation existed between two entities such as near and far, big and small, or hot and cold; is called relation and can be utilized to teach and enhance the principle of connection or relationship. *Relation* is necessary to provide more complex matrix for further cognitive production such as *system, transformation,* and *implication* (Guilford, 1977). These processes are more complex forms of presenting information to our cognitive domain. Consequently, the more your toddler engages with the play the more responses and functional relationships will be produced and eventually, the pattern of thought gains creative characteristics.

Chapter Five

COGNITIVE DOMAIN
IN INFANCY & TODDLERHOOH

Stages of Cognition

Cognition is a set of interrelated processes which enables the brain to make sense of its inner and outer surroundings. There are many different definition of cognition. But all of the definitions have several commonalities. In fact, cognition can be defined as all the processes by which humans acquire knowledge; or methods for thinking or gaining knowledge about the world (Seifert & Hoffnung, 2000). Cognition involves many different brain activities, says: "many of which are undiscovered by man." From what we know so far, cognition includes thinking, learning, perceiving, memory, remembering, understanding, and creativity. Based on the present knowledge, cognitive development submits to the growth and refinement of these intellectual processes (Craig & Dunn, 2007).

In infancy and toddler-hood stages, humans start subsistence thinking. Children in this age use *sensory* perception and *motor* action to interact with objects in the environment around them (Seifert & Hoffnung, 2000). This process is known as the *sensorimotor intelligence*. Basically, infants demonstrate two inclinations as they grow older; symbolic thinking and an explicit cognitive structure which particularly belongs to this exact age. In symbolic thinking infants develop capabilities that help them to have some symbolic point of reference for an object in their minds. Through visualization or thinking about that object without having that object in front of them they have a name; for example: a key. This capability of visualization or thinking about an object, in the absence of that entity increases as they grow older. Additionally, in this phase of development infants form cognitive structures which are organized patterns that aid them in making sense of the world around them and help them in adapting to the surroundings.

According to Piaget, children interpret new incoming information through two structural avenues known as *assimilation* and *accommodation.* Through assimilation, the infant processes information in the course of the existing structure. During the process of accommodation the infant has to modify the existing structure in order to decode the incoming information. The interchange of these two processes creates a *new structure* and eventually the infant becomes able to symbolize the object or think about the object in the absence of that particular object. Based on Piaget's theory of intelligence humans goes through four distinctive *stages:* Sensorimotor, Preoperational, Concrete-Operational, and Formal. Each stage has different *contents* which are designed to collectively characterize that particular stage.

The sensorimotor stage consists of six factors, imitation, circular reaction, time, object concept, causality, and space. These contents help the infant to form an early concept of objects, people and self. As a result, the cognitive content of a newborn moves from disorganized, reflexive, and self-centered to an organized content that is well adapted to the environment (Bee & Boyd, 2009). Considering the six factors of the sensorimotor stage, infants and toddlers steer through six cognitive shifts. These shifts are known as sub-stage.

Cognitive activities

All of the activities during the periods of infancy and toddlerhood are divided into the different age range. Since each age bracket has its own specific content and function, the process of maturity becomes the focus of purposed activities. These activities are tailored to strengthen the present structure of each sub-stage and facilitate the advancement and sustainability of these learned materials.

Early Reflexes: Sub-Stage One

Early Reflexes starts at ages 0-1 month. Early reflexes determine the infant's neurological network processing with the environment. These simple reflexes are conjectured to govern the majority of intellectual behaviors, but some psychologists are at odds with this idea. They think infants are more capable of reflexive responses (Brainerd, 1978). These reflexes are the early nucleus of vital behaviors such as eating, and locomotion. In this sub-stage, infants connect with objects and the environment as long as they are exposed to it. In other words "out of sight, out of mind".

Activities to consider

Activity I. Facilitate sensory discrimination through repetition and adaptation. In this activity, you simultaneously expose the newborn to two different stimulations. First, during bathing, you gently place the right hand fingers of the newborn in water that is 20 degrees cooler than the bath water. Keep the hand there for 5 seconds and then place it back in regular bath water. When you place the newborn's hand in the cooler water, you can whistle and when you place it back in the bath water you can hum. This sensory differentiation mixed with auditory association creates the ability for the child to *differentiate*. Later on, alternates humming with whistling during non-bath activities; and see if the baby shows any reflexive responses. Whether he shows any responses or not, you are exercising the primal notion of memorization.

Activity II. Choose three different toys and show them to the infant for a period of 10 seconds each. Make sure they are different colors and are placed not further than six inches from the infant's face. This helps the child differentiate between objects.

Activity III. In a desirable room temperature allow the child to be uncovered. This condition creates an opportunity for the infant to move her/his limbs around without restrictions.

Activity IV. Allow bare skin cuddling of your baby (Clark, 2007). This allows the infant to bond with you and assists them in recognizing your texture and sent.

Primary Circular Reaction: Sub-stage Two

Primary Circular Reaction (Brainerd, 1978) starts around ages 1-4 months. In this period some of the early reflexes are modified and repetitive behaviors are substitutes. Usually infants at this age start to rotate their arms over and over or move their limbs in one direction. Generally, infants begin to perform in a more coordinated action. In the previous sub-stage, actions were separate, but in this sub-stage actions are coordinated. This integration of activities has a repetitive quality.

Incorporating different senses such as auditory and visual is important during the second and third months. The more complex frontal cortex activities are the more eye-hand coordination is needed. Therefore, exercises geared toward incorporating visual and auditory channels can facilitate the growth of cognitive functioning, in this junction.

Mid cerebellum formation and reticular formation during, the second and third months, allows for regulation and control of muscle tone with the coordination of voluntary movements (Sutton-Smith, 1973). It is important to know that this developmental time for mid-cerebellum and reticular formation encourages the voluntarily movements of the muscle in limbs (Feldman, 2007). On the other hand, creative imagination requires conveying information between several neural pathways; the limbic system and the cortex (Silverman, 2000). Therefore, cultivating these pathways in the earlier part of life may increases the synaptic connections. Sagan (1977) estimated that people process only several trillion bits of information through his/her life span but we do not use more than 5% of our brain capacity

(Ferguson, 1973). Thus, the early stimulation may enhance this statistics

Activities to consider

Activity I. Encourage grasping objects and toys. Place your finger in the infant's palm and allow him/her to grasp it. After the infant grasps your finger, try to gently pull it out. The resistance the infant shows in preventing your finger from leaving his/her palm is a good facilitator for cognitive development.

Activity II. Provide a safe object for the infant to suck on.

Activity III. Each time you introduce an object to the child; name the object and slowly repeat the name of the object. Continue naming the object four times. Let the infant see your facial expressions, while you name the object. By showing the one object at time and naming the object to the newborn the first nucleus of intellectual functioning starts to immerge.

Activity IV. The infant at these two months is capable of understanding the concept of space in relation with action (Sutton-Smith, 1973). That means when the infant rattles the noise-making toy, she can have the concept of objects in space because he/she hears the noise or sees the movement. For this activity you should use toys that make moderate noise and are accessible to the infant to touch. The weight should be light enough to create movement. You need to be careful with the size and the hazardous condition of the toys. Infants have the habit of instinctually examining objects through their mouth. Therefore, all the toys and materials should be safe and big enough not to be swallowed by the infant.

Activity V. Change the position of the baby's bed and changing table in the room to allow maximum exposure of different stimuli.

Activity VI. Infants in this phase are able to show *deferred imitation*, (Sutton-Smith, 1973), capable of storing information in memory and retrieving it at the different times. To strengthen the memory, you should get close to the infant and talk to the baby and make sure the baby sees your facial movement. Make sure that facial expressions are accompanied with appropriate vocal expressions (the correct affect and feeling should be implemented). Usually the infant imitates mouth and eye movements first (Sutton-Smith, 1973), but the combination of emotional input adds to the quality of learned bits of information.

Activity VII. Place patterns with a verity of shapes and colors above the child's crib (Clark, 2007).

Secondary Circular Reactions: Sub-stage Three

Secondary Circular Reactions (Brainerd, 1978) starts between ages 4-8 months. They are less reflexive than primary circular reactions. These behaviors are generally discovered by accident (Brainerd, 1978). During these months attention is shifted from the infant's body to the surroundings and action is used as means toward the ends. This is the first sign of *object permanency* which involves direct action on the object (Feldman, 2007).

Activities to consider

Activity I. Expose the infant to picture books with shapes, color, letters, and some simple words. When showing these picture books, speak slowly and in adult dialogue with the infant. Read the illustrated baby books when she/he is resting or before going to sleep. Bring to her/his attention the pictures of those objects and animals that she/he heard before for reinforcing the learning and rehearsing from long-term memory.

Activity II. Play the peek-a-boo game. This activity provides skills in auditory and visual problem solving. It also supports transformation and anticipation skills. These skills are fundamental to future enhancement of *logical sequencing*.

Activity III. Give the baby a bottle of milk or juice and allow the infant to try to place it in mouth. If the infant holds the bottle with both hands, try to help him hold it with one. As he is holding the bottle with one hand, engage the other hand to something totally different. Alternate the hands with this activity.

Activity IV. The second circular reaction can be encouraged and mastered during this phase. When the infant moves the object during this developmental phase, she starts with random touching and moving. Gradually, it becomes a purposeful and more sophisticated intellectual act, which is not considered random. Attractive and moveable objects that can slide from side to side should be placed above the baby's bed, where the infant can reach and manipulate them.

Activity V. Place three simple toys of one kind (three stuffed animals) and one different object (red ball) in front of the infant in the same area. First tell the infant that you are going to put these three stuffed animals together and keep the red ball in a different place (child has to be able to see all four objects). By just showing the infant, you help the infant to understand the basic concept of classification and relation. Later on, leave the toys with her and encourage her to repeat the procedures.

Activity VI. Take a stuffed animal toy and pretend that you are feeding the toy animal with a spoon. Then, ask the infant to feed the toy animal.

Activity VII. During bathing, you should fill up the bathtub to half. Hold the infant at the waist and after checking the desirable water temperature; place her gently in the water. Keep pulling her in and out several times for a few second in between until she feels the sensation of gravity. Do not put the infant's under the water. Make sure you observe all of the safety features when you performing this or any of the exercises.

Activity VIII. Name different parts of body, while the infant is on the changing table. Mix this activity with laughter to make it interesting to the infant.

[Verbal encouragement and personal attention is vitally important]

Coordination of Secondary Circular Reactions: Sub-stage Four

Coordination of Sensory Circular Reaction (Brainerd, 1978) starts between ages 8-12 months. The infant starts to use a more calculated approach to producing events (Feldman, 2007) and this increases decision making skills. The process of means-end connections becomes *purposefully* applied. In this sub-stage the infant begins to deploy goal-directed behavior through the utilization of several solitary acts. This step of acting purposefully is obtained after the step of acting accidentally (sub-stage 3). The exercises in this section are designed to teach the child to move from disorganized random search to an organized an effective search pattern.

Activities to consider

Activity I. Place four matching color spoons and wooden blocks in front of the child. First, group all the spoons together on one side and blocks on the others. Allow the child to look at them. If she wants to play with them she is permitted to do so. Then repeat this classification of spoons and blocks two more times. As you classifying them, tell the child "the spoon goes with the spoons and the block goes with the block". Then mix them and ask the child to separate the spoons from the blocks. Continue this until the child becomes fluent.

Activity II. Provide a safe and unbreakable mirror for this activity. Point to the different parts of child's body such as head, hand, or foot in front of the mirror. As you point to the different body parts you should name them. Then ask the child to show you those parts on the mirror's surface.

Activity III. Mix a couple pieces of your infant's favorite fruit with two big objects (toys). Make sure the toys are big enough that the infant can not swallow them. Then place the bowl containing the fruits and big objects, in front of him. You should not guide or give any direction to the child; let him to differentiate edible from non-edibles. This activity should be applied while it is close to his meal time. With this activity he learns to move from disorganized random search to an organized effective search pattern. This exercise should be repeated once a day for two months. Then each time he finishes his favorite piece of fruit, asks him "where has the fruit gone?" This portion of activity enhances four different skills at the same time: visualization, intuition, decision-making, and imagination enhancement.

Activity IV. Play the counting game (one, two, buckle my shoe) to teach basic arithmetic (Eisenberg, Murkoff, & Hathaway, 1989).

Activity V. Hide a toy under a red cloth as the child is watching. Ask the child to retrieve the toy. Then, hide a toy under the red cloth again, as the child watching. Wait for three seconds, then take the toy from beneath of the red cloth and transfer it under the white cloth (without allowing the child see the transferring the toy). Ask the child to find the toy. If the child looks for the toy under the red cloth, explain to him and guide him to look under the white cloth. Repeat the process until the child learns that the toy is under the white cloth.

Activity VI. Read to the child at least every two hours for five to fifteen minutes. For this activity you should use different illustrated children's books. In favor of language development, you should encourage conversation by immediately asking questions about what you have read to the child. You should avoid baby talk and speak clearly, fluently, and appropriately. Repeat the same procedures at night, before the child goes to sleep. Listening to soft music during night reading is recommended.

Tertiary Circular Reactions: Sub-Stage Five

Tertiary Circular Reactions (Brainerd, 1978) start to appear between ages of 12 to 18 months. This is a phase of discovery and *active experimentation*. The toddler uses trial and error to learn about the environment. In this period, the toddler is not any more interested to act up on the object for sheer enjoyment. He fascinated to carry out small experiments and to examine the consequences.

The toddler is capable of mental representation. Since the child is capable of moving from trial and error phase of mental operation to symbolic representation, the mental processing develops into internalizing ability. Therefore, more information will transfer to long-term memory and more connective bonds will be formed between memory bits. In other words, there is a symbolic reference in the child's mind beside the perceptual representation of an object. For example, the child knows the *word* chair besides the mental picture of the chair. This symbolic scheme helps the child to deal with his environment in a *subjective* manner as well as an *objective* mode. Furthermore, in this age, the object exists not only because of its action but also because of its mental representation.

The second monumental progress in cognitive development during this age bracket is the ability to suspend *imitation* of an observed event until later. This delayed imitation of observed events creates a symbolic connotation which fuels creativity.

The way this evolves is that physical imitation of an event submerges to a symbolic imitation, creating a new mental coding system known as language. Based on the toddlers memory capacity the child arrives at a new and creative response in the form of language.

Another distinct intellectual advancement in this sub-stage is persuasion. In this particular phase of development the child becomes interested in pursuing invisible objects after being hidden. Previously, the object ceased to exist as soon as the object was removed from the perceptual field. When some one hides the object, the child stops looking for it. Now at this age the toddler can take account of visible and invisible objects and looks for the object in many different places (Craig & Dunn, 2007). This new maturity initiates the fresh mental references known as *hunches*. Among many advantages of this newly formed skill, the reflection before action develops healthy self-confidence for the toddler.

Cognition shift

When the mental operation shifts from *discovery* to *invention* the new means through usage of memory begins to form. This internal composition empowers the toddler to move from *systematic imitation* of new action to *internalizing* that action. This giant step is the beginning of formation of intelligent memory with stable connectivity. Whereas about age 1, the only memory was ordinary, around 18 months the connectivity of pieces of memory strengthen. Between 18 and 24 months the toddler become equipped to use symbolic means to recall the contents of intelligent memory.

Activities to consider

Activity I. Place your child in his high chair or somewhere stable. Place a toy animal and his juice cup in front him. Then ask him to give you the juice cup. After the several successive trials change the command and ask him to give you that toy. Then ask the child to put the toy in the cup. Repeat this exercise several times until the child gains the mastery of double commands. Repeat this exercise with other objects while he is moving around the room. This activity teaches the child the transition of cognitive processing from trial and error to representation.

Activity II. Show the child her favorite toy. Then take away the toy and hide it somewhere near by, not further than ten feet. Next ask the child to go and find the hidden toy.

Activity III. Encourage the child to speak and talk about different objects around the house in more than one sentence.

Activity IV. Start to teach the child colors, letters, numbers and several simple words. Additionally, encourage the child to identify parts of his/her body through the mirror and allow him to identify yours in the mirror as well.

Activity V. Let the child bend and ask him/her to explain the surrounding environment when he sees the world up side down.

Invention of New Means through Mental Combinations: Sub-stage Six

Invention of New Means through Mental Combinations occurs between ages of 16 to 24 months (Brainerd, 1978). This sub-stage is known as the beginning of thought and deliberate contemplation. The capacity of thought and language begin to emerge in the form of mental representation (Feldman, 2007). Another developmental milestone in the cognitive domain is playing pretend games. Children are able to play *pretend* games, such as pretending that they are riding a horse when they are sitting on a pillow. For the first time the toddler begin to use the notion of imagination and becomes infatuated with creativity. The toddlers imagine and envision the action and it results without actually having to try them out in advance (Seifert & Hoffnung, 2000).

One of the fundamental tasks of this sensorimotor stage is causality. The role of causality in the form of expectancy aids the cognitive behavior to interexchange between two brain hemispheres (Yazdani, 1984). Considering the different functioning of each hemisphere (left and right), the notion of causality becomes extremely important in formation and also inhibition of creativity.

Causality

The relationship between cause and effect is vital in the formation of logical thinking. This relationship promotes the recall of long-term memory bits in restructuring new information. Piaget views causality as a capacity to anticipate what consequences will follow from a certain action or what cause probably produced a particular result. This phenomenon of causality begins to form in the sixth sub-stage (Piaget, 1975). After the development of causality, individual eventually is able to draw logical conclusions from bits of information. There are two aspects of cause and effect. One is physical which is purely objective in nature; and the other is psychological which is subjective and refers to one's action, influenced by some *wish*. Children at the sixth sub-stage are only capable of understanding physical causality and have no inclination about psychological causality.

By now the child has already learned that by banging the spoon on the table or some surface, he can make the noise. This example of cause and effect can be generalized for other relationships and the child can anticipate some effect by imagining the banging of the spoon on the surface. This brings a realization for toddlers that two events which occur closely together should be somehow related to each other.

Activities to consider

Activity I. Encourage make-better-play as much as possible.

Activity II. Place a child at the table and put a ball in front of her. First show her that the ball can be rolled by pushing. Then encourage the child to push the ball and experience the rolling action.

Activity III. Repeat activity one with one minor modification. This time, place the ball on the 30-degree ramp and release the ball from the top of the ramp without pushing. Encourage the child to repeat the activity.

Concept of object

The object concept refers to a general belief that people, places, and things continue to exist when we are no longer in direct contact with them (Piaget, 1978). This concept continues its maturation through the sixth sub-stage and into the second year of life. A toddler in the living room can grasp the idea that the voice coming from the kitchen is his mother's voice; though he can not see her in the living room. During the last six months of the second year, the concept of object shifts from looking where the object was hidden to looking for objects in different places. This full-blown object concept gives the toddler the ability to take account of invisible and visible displacement. The child actively involves himself in searching in probable places to find others.

Activities to consider

Activity I. Play a game of hide and seek with the child.

Activity II. Ask the child to imitate different animal's sound.

Activity III. Ask the child to go to his room and bring you different objects. If he can not find it, encourage him to look for it

Association

In this age the child has the capability to associate two pieces of information together and draw a logical response (*convergent thinking*); one problem generates only one solution.

Activities to consider

Activity I. Challenge the child to make animal sound, natural noises, and what ever she has been hearing. Then ask her to make a different noise for cats or dogs.

Activity II. Ask the child to identify different colors and then ask him to choose the crayon that is the same color as the sky, grass, and so on.

> Q1. What color is the sky?
> Q2. What color is the grass?
> Q3. What color is your (favorite toy)?

Make sure you ask questions which deal with auditory memory and simple facts around the house.

Language development

Language development in this phase takes place mostly in latency. There is compelling evidence that toddlers in this age bracket absorb linguistics including grammar and words. However, they are not able to repeat as many words as they absorb (Sutton-Smith, 1973). The rapidly developing cognitive abilities require many mental symbols. This gives a vast capability first to store and secondly, to verbally recall the stored materials. Language as a symbolic vehicle forms the transition of memory bits to the verbal representation of those bits.

According to some findings, toddlers at age 24 months possess an extensive vocabulary of 270 words (Sutton-Smith, 1973). The formation of sentences in this age bracket is mostly two word sentences, like "baby go". This simple two word sentence, "baby go" has several meanings: baby is going, I want to go, other baby has gone, or so on. It is astonishing to know that her verbal capacity for next two years, may reach over 1500 words.

Activities to consider

Activity I. During your casual conversation with your toddler, try to show her the objects that you use in your conversation. It allows your child to rehearse her ordinary memory. The effect of learning increases if the child sees your mouth movement. To accomplish this you need to encourage your child to look at you during conversations.

Activity II. Let your child sit in front of mirror and talk to herself while you are standing next to her.

Activity III. Read books with illustrated pictures and more complex verbal content before bed or during playtime. After finishing these short stories ask the toddler to read the same story; most of the time the toddler either memorizes the story or just repeats it in her own way. Either scenario is acceptable.

Chapter Six

PSYCHOSOCIAL DEVELOPMENT IN INFANCY & TODDLERHOOD

Emotional Growth

Mothers and care-givers are the first most important persons in the infant's psycho-social development. Following birth, a newborn infant who was in the isolation of the mother's womb is capable of several basic social interactions. For example; he/she can cry and get another human being involves in his/her need fulfilling process. A few months later, the child can smile and interact with few people around. Given that the infant grows so does the amount of socialization.

In the first couple months of life the infant's reflexive responses becomes more autonomous. This transition from reflexive responses to autonomous response generates *skills*. Lifting head, smiling, and pushing toys around, becomes more the means of expression of inner drives than simple reflexive movement. Communication via cognitive and emotive domains begins to represent the individuality of the infant. In the midst of these interactions, feeling, drive, motivation, and locus of control starts to interact in specific ways based on the genetic make up and environmental influences. In other words the personality immerges.

With the first sign of language the aim of socialization moves from centering on the infant to more socially popular responses; mostly influenced by culture, tradition, parental value and other factors.

All of these interactions create a unique dynamic of responding and interpreting the world for the child.

One of the early and important notions in human psycho-social development is *attachment*. The initial bond is assumed to be formed in the first couple hours after birth between newborn infant and the mother. The nature of this attachment, the issues surrounding this connection between infant and the mother or care giver, determines the future foundations of the child's personality, socialization, and coping structure. If the attachment is secure the psychological consequences in the future are promising. On the other hand, if the attachment is insecure the psychological outcomes are damaging. Nevertheless, the impact of bonding or attachment in the early part of life plays an important role in the psychological functioning. Table 6.1 shows the four stages of attachment formation.

Stages of Attachment Formation

Stages	Attachment formation
I. Birth-2 months: Indiscriminate Sociability	Uses limited attachment behaviors toward parents, less selective,
II. 2-7 months: Attachments in the making.	Increase preference for individual most familiar and responsive to needs
III. 8-24 months: Specific Attachment	Preference for specific people
IV. 24 months onward: Goal-coordinated Partnership	Tolerate short separation from parents, cooperation with others,

Table 6.1 Source: Bowlby (1969)

Achieving novelty and originality by a creative or gifted mind requires a psychological atmosphere, free from inhibition, secure and unchained to valuing diversity. This can't easily be attained unless the initial social bonding and trusting mechanism of *self* has been properly formed. To build sufficient trust to synthesize and analyze incoming information from outside of self requires an attitude, free from apprehension to *"unknowns"*. This status can not be achieved unless the secure attachment had been formed.

Emotion and temperament in first two years of life

The research shows an array of complexity in infant and toddler's emotions (Seifert & Huffnung, 2000). An infant, a few days old is capable of producing facial expressions, particularly the negative emotion such as frowning. By three months they can generate joy and even guilt and envy by toddlerhood. Table 6.2 shows the development of emotional milestones during the first 24 months.

Emotional Millstone in the First Two Year

Age Range in Month	Emotion	Psychosocial Stage of Development
0-1	Social Smile	Trust versus mistrust
3	Pleasure Smile	Trust versus mistrust
3-4	Wariness	Trust versus mistrust
4-7	Joy, anger, sadness	Trust versus mistrust
4	Surprise	Trust versus mistrust
5-9	Fear	Trust versus mistrust
10-18	Shame	Autonomy versus Shame and doubt
19-24	Contempt, guilt	Autonomy versus Shame and doubt

Table 6.2 Development of infant emotion & psychosocial stages of development, Sources: Izard (1994): Lewis (1992); Erikson, 1982

As the cognitive domain develops the emotional responses become more complex.

One of the valuable donors to better understanding human emotion is the priceless contribution of Erik Erikson. According to Erik Erikson (1982), in the early part of life, the infant goes through a psychosocial crisis known as *trust versus mistrust*. In this crisis the dichotomy rests on the idea that whether the infant can rely on the caregiver to reliably meet his/her physical and emotional needs. Between age two and three the toddler faces another psychosocial crisis known as *autonomy versus shame and doubt*. This crisis involves the struggle to control one's thoughts, feelings and actions. *Autonomy* refers to the toddler's capacity to balance personal demands in favor of self-control with the demands on behalf of parent-controls. *Shame* involves a loss of self-respect due to failure to meet one's own standards (Lewis, 1992).

The early social relationships of infants and toddlers require a healthy pattern of closely coordinated social interaction. Signs such as gazing, cooing, smiling, and later on speech become the means of communication in collective situations. As child grows from infancy to toddlerhood and beyond, the interaction with peers become more crucial. Particularly, the toddlers who spend time at day care centers. The research shows better and more sophisticated social skills are produced by the infants and toddlers who spend time in well functioning day cares.

Concept of Self

One of the early challenges for humans is the exertion of self control over their own life. Self evaluation is an instinctual act for humans. As we constantly evaluate our position in conjunction with other people and the physical world around us, we arrive at our position of identity. Sets of pervasive and detailed ideas about ourselves, our identity, and the world around us are called self-concept. Generally, self-concept begins with physical self-recognition, self awareness, self-description and self-evaluation, followed by knowledge of standards and emotional responses to wrongdoing (Kochansky et al., 1998; Stipek et al., 1990). Since the formation of self-concept has its cognitive and emotive roots; the impression of self-concept becomes a tendency to achieve authentic beings (Hall & Lindzey, 1985), strive to superiority or perfection (1956), or a tendency to enhance of life (Maslow, 1954).

In the beginning, the world around the infant is not a separate entity from self. In other words, the only entity that existed in the very early part of life is *me* and nothing else exists independent of *me*. As humans grow beyond toddlerhood the interaction between *me* and the world outside of *me* develops and gradually the child realizes there is *you*. Finally, as the organism grows the human becomes aware that the involved parties are not only *me* or *you* but there are *others* as well. Therefore, the concept of self goes through many different levels of involvement. This involvement helps humans to realize his/ her positions with respect to others and expanding the elements of the world, me, you, and others.

Some psychologists explained the concept of self as a symbolic relationship between the mother and the infant in which they are joined together as one entity capable of becoming separated (Freud, 1930). This first step of transition becomes stronger as the infant starts to receive help from the mother or caregiver. For example, about age16 to 18 months, when the infant throws the toy off the table or smiles back to the mother through the process of getting the toy back, he learns that this extended part of self has a separate identity.

The first phase of understanding of self as a separated entity starts about age one to one and half (Bee & Boyd, 2009). Though the babies around age 9 to 12 months old can look in the mirror and make faces at themselves and become aware of the basic abilities to interact with self, they can't realize that it is their own image. They think it is the image of another baby. Some of psychologists believe that babies around age 21 months old can recognize that the image in the mirror is their image. Other research indicates that when the infant is around age 15 to 18 months he sees his own image on video or observes his picture and starts to smile. This ability usually starts at the same time the infant are able to grasp the object (Bee & Boyd, 2009).

These shifts indicate that around 15 to 18 months the baby starts to identify the concept of *"beside me."* Interestingly, the complete recognition of self and others becomes fully recognizable by ages 18 to 24 months. This developmental phase of self concept regarding to the size, age, and gender becomes significantly noticeable due to the shift of cognitive development from *reflex activity* to *representation*. This brings a radical shift from the egocentric mode of operation to the altruistic mode.

Psychosocial Activities

All the activities during infancy and toddlerhood are divided into different age ranges due to specific characteristics of each age bracket. Maturity and capability of each stage content and structure are respected and carefully analyzed for advanced intervention and sustainability of learned materials.

Age 0 to 2 months

As early as the moment after birth, the newborn's personality starts shaping through interactions with the mother and the demands of the newborn's organism. Physiological needs must be fulfilled, environmental factors begin to bombard the infant, and the physical world impacts the organism. All of these factors embark on shaping the personality of this new arrival. As long as the brain operation is involved, at the very beginning, most activities are reflexive. The infant is totally governed by reflexes and has a 100% dependence on the care giver. Therefore, the manner in which the care has been rendered plays an important role in the psycho-social development of child. Limited physical movements, fresh metabolically processes and brand new physiological functioning of the newborns start to play a role on the perceived quality of care. Since the newborn organism is vulnerable to many environmental factors and has a total dependency on the mother, the manners in which the needs are met become the subject of survival and security.

If the physiological safety and security needs (Maslow, 1954) of child have not been properly met, the impact of such a poor fulfillment would effect the emotional functioning of the child throughout his life span. One of the important blocks to healthy personality formation is the *attachment* issue. In this early age, the visual interaction between newborn and the mother provides the first block to strong attachment. Therefore, the manner in which, the basic needs of baby were fulfilled and the fashion of attending to these needs creates a basic road map for attachment formation and consequently the personality development of the newborn.

Activities to consider

Activity I. After feeding allow the baby to burp. By gently rubbing the infant's stomach and talking to him/her you provide the first nucleus of healthy attachment. This activity also releases the gastrointestinal tensions. Newborns have a brand new gastrointestinal track and this track is not accustomed to food, therefore the reduction of tension creates a feeling of comfort for newborns. This activity also produces an accepting and secure feeling.

Activity II. From the first couple days after birth to the first year, the infant's challenge is acclimating to the effect of the gravity force on the body and the notion of balance. While holding, support the neck and body of newborn. This helps the newborn to gradually adapt to the effect of gravity. This provides the first physical core of safety and security through equilibrium. Avoid sudden and jerky movements because the unfamiliar sensation of imbalance can be anxiety-provoking. Always observe safety and common sense when you are handling your child.

Activity III. During cuddling, playing, or changing the baby's clothes or diaper get as close as possible to the baby's face and let her/him touch your face. She can use the sense of smell and vision to bond with you. Changing of diaper and remove urine and feces from the newborn's sensitive skin promotes a sense of security and advocates comfort and belonging. Thus, each time the newborn requires the care, the opportunity for bonding, socialization, and promotion of appropriate social responses emerges.

Activity IV. Feed the child and change the diaper on a regular schedule. These routine performances provide more stability and fulfill the child's expectation and gives security to the child. Feeding and changing on schedule establishes the early expectation of discipline and order.

Age 2 to 4 months

Between ages two to four months the infant is more adjusted to the environment and is capable of feeling content, joy, surprised and fear (Snow, 1998). According to Erikson the major psychosocial crisis for the infant begins around age one month through the first year. During the first year of life, children experience their first psychosocial developmental crisis; *trust versus mistrust*. The psychosocial crisis of children involves whether they can rely on their parents to meet their physical and emotional needs (Seifert, Huffnung, 2000). The resolution in this stage aids the child in learning self-trust (hope).

In this phase, the most biological functioning of infants are vegetation behaviors (eating, sleeping, and growing). Proper room and water temperature during bathing, colic pains and other related issues should be carefully monitored. This monitoring contributes to the healthy development of safety and security (Maslow, 1954). Fulfilling the infants' basic needs such as feeding, urinating and defecating, sleep and pain management must be in a prudent fashion. Parents should deal with sense of urgency, patient, free from exaggerated reaction, and mixed with at the most caring manners. When ever the mother removes any discomfort, she should verbalize the action in a calm and composed tone of voice and body language. Though the baby does not understand the meaning of those spoken words and sentences, intuitively she can establish enough trust in an anxiety free environment to promote the sense of security and acceptance.

Activities to consider

Activity I. Allow bare skin cuddling; rub baby's skin with towel when drying; tickle, squeeze gently; hand out "feely" objects, e.g., velvet, silk, sponge. Turn lights on and off to provide visual stimulation (Clark, 2007).

Activity II. Alter the position of the child during bottle feeding, change the location of cribs in the room, and vary the hanging toys over the crib. These changes increase the hemispheric coordination, memory pool, visual stimulation, and visual complexity.

Activity III. Hang some toys with specific characteristics. Hanging toys should be bright colors, complex shapes, and safe. The parts should be hung with semi rigid attached (not string) that allows motion to occur. No sharp, loud, or abrupt changes in stimulation such as flashing lights (Clark, 2007).

Activity IV. Play the game of "This-Little-Piggy". This game is more than entertainment. Love, nearness, touch and giving and receiving contented emotions improves socialization and bonding.

Activity V. In order to feel safe, secure and self-reliant; mother, father, educators, friends, and other people in the house should play some social games with the infant. These games should be geared toward improving group participation.

Age 5-9 months

During this age the child is capable of some physical movement such as crawling and handling objects in hand. Additionally, the objects around the room can be seen easier than before due to improvement in vision and better ability through hand manipulations. Infants are more capable of showing their emotions through expression. One of the ear marks of this age is expression of rage (Snow, 1998). Due to expansion of memory the child is capable of associating past events to the quality of present need execution and express joy or anger in a more systematic fashion. Since the core of psychosocial development in children in the first year of life is trust versus mistrust, the dependability on the parents brings about personality strength or *virtue* (Seifert, Huffnung, 2000).

Activities to consider

Activity I. Respond to infant's signals and reactions by verbal acknowledgment, expressive and appropriate body language, and meaningful interactions during the awakening hours. This strengthens the capacity of trust and ultimately empowers the internal locus of control.

Activity II. Respond to distress signals of infants in a patient and calm manner. This establishes a code of mutual expectancy.

Activity III. Provide a variety of sounds with variety of rhythms.

Activity IV. Imitate the baby's cooing with proper facial and emotional expressions.

Activity V. Introduce emotional words such as "happy" "wondered" "puzzled", "Sad", and so on. As you using these words make sure you show the proper facial expression, corresponding to the presented emotion or word.

Activity VI. Let the baby play with safe toys that are patterned, manipulative and textured. This stimulates self-initiation activities (Clark, 2007).

Age 10 to 18 months

The child is practically mobile and can go a lot of places around the house. Emotional expression such as love and empathy starts to manifest itself in this age bracket (Snow, 1998). Acting in a morally responsible fashion, aids the child to develop a healthy ethical sense. Children judge you based on your performance. They model their interactions with their surroundings based on what they viewed from you, as a model.

The psychosocial crisis during the second year of life is a dilemma of balancing the child's demands for self control versus the demands of being controlled by parents or others. This crisis is known as *autonomy versus shame and doubt* (Erikson, 1982).

Children in this age bracket develop control over their body functioning and have a capability to independently direct their activities. The healthy completion of this stage leads to having a *strong will.*

Activities to consider

Activity I. Encourage the child to have a sense of humor. The best way to teach a child is modeling. Laugh a lot around the child.

Activity II. Teach the child to be respectful toward toys and possessions.

Activity III. Use a lot of verbal praise and hugs and kisses when a child accomplishes any small task.

Activity IV. Allow the child to feel the sunshine, wind, and listen to different sounds of nature.

Activity V. Provide situations that allow the child to solve simple problems. After these accomplishments allow the rest of family to view them and periodically talk about that in front of the child.

Activity VI. Play a game by asking the child to show different emotional expressions through facial and vocal expressions.

Activity VII. Allow some private time for the toddler.

Activity VIII. In this essential stage, learning about the consequences of their acts is important. Though the caregiver may think that the child is not old enough to understand complicated vocabulary, you should not restrain yourself in explaining why a certain response is not acceptable. Say "yes" and "no" consistently and clearly without compromising. Additionally, set boundaries and explain the consequences of their actions in short sentences.

Activity IX. Never praise the child when he/she did not perform according to your acceptable criteria. This irrelevant reinforcing confuses the child and undervalues the potency of reward. The proper application of reward helps to accept and value the concept of *discipline*.

Age 18 to 24 months

By 18 to 24 months, the toddler is a sociable individual with a capability of understanding pride, shame, embarrassment and guilt. There is a deeper understanding of interpersonal relationships with others at this age and the child can interact with other people. The child is no longer the center of existence and the toddler knows the concept of *me* and *you* as two separate entities. The child can delay upon request and begin to behave according to social expectations in the absence of external monitoring (Seifert, Huffnung, 2000).

Activities to consider

Activity I. Have a discussion with the child about the daily activities in the house.

Activity II. Ask the child's input for food and other simple activities around the house.

Activity III. Provide a set schedule for eating, sleeping, and down time for the toddler.

Activity IV. Brain-storm with the child in regard to how other members of family should feel in some emotional situations.

Activity V. Give some simple and safe assignment to the child and teach the child how he/she can work in collaboration with others. Celebrate these accomplishments.

Activity VI. Give some assignment to the child to handle without collaboration and celebrate the accomplishment.

Activity VII. Periodically, ask the opinion of the child; leave some room for creativity.

Activity VIII. Encourage the child to come up with a simple skit and let the child direct the skit, using family members for acting.

Activity IX. Never praise the child when he/she did not perform up to the task. This confuses the child and undervalues the potency of reward.

Activity X. Teach the toddler to wait his turn. Have the family or other people gather together and each take a turn to doing something special. Make sure while one is performing, the others just listen or observe without infringing on the performer. Your child should be in the group and be asked to do the same. No matter how irrelevant or relevant the child's performance is, others need to acknowledge and respect the child.

Activity XI. Take the child to as many different social functions as possible. Allow him/her to play with other children in the park, play ground and other places that you deemed safe.

Chapter Seven

PHYSICAL DEVELOPMENT IN EARLY CHILDHOOD

Physical Growth

The extent of life from age two to six is known as early childhood or the preschool range. Two years after birth, the average weight for the average child in the United State is about 25-30 pounds and he is close to 36 inches tall. Since children grow progressively during early childhood, by the time they are six years old, they weight, on average, about 46 pounds and stand 46 inches (Feldman, 2007). Most dimensions of growth are influenced by genetics, the height and weight of parents plays some role in the size of their off spring. Other factors influencing physical development of children are nutrition and diseases. By following the scheduled immunization and balanced nutrition the proper physical growth of children can be safeguarded. Preschool children do not require as many calories per unit of their body weight as they did instantaneously after birth. What they need most in this phase is a variety of food. Providing a discipline for healthy eating at this age range can become a reliable model for a healthy life ahead.

Brain Development

By age three the brain size and weight is about 75% of adult size and by age five 90%. In comparison, the average 5-year-old's total body weight is just 30% of the average adult's body weight (Nihart, 1993). Beginning in this phase, the brain starts to function physically in adult like ways (Seifert & Huffnung, 2000), but, cognitively it has to go through several additional processes.

The human brain is clearly a double organ consisting of two similar looking hemispheres joined together by several bundles of nerve fibers, responsible for communication between the left and right brain hemispheres. This bundle of fibers is known as the *corpus callosum* (Blakeslee, 1937). Lateralization or propensity for the left and right hemispheres of the brain to execute separately immerges in the early childhood phase of development. Each hemisphere has its own separate train of conscious thought and its own memory (Sperry, 1968). The right brain thinks directly in sensory images. In general the left brain is responsible for analyzing incoming information, breaking it into understandable path; and the right brain is responsible for synthesizing the information.

Left Brain	Right Brain
Analytic	Synthetic
Comparative	Holistic
Logical	Imagery
Relational	Intuitive
Technological and scientific	Artistic and humanistic
Breaks down the content	Gathers together the pieces
Digital	Gestalt

The role of right brain functioning in the production of creative imagery and the utilization of creativity has been the bed rock of many arguments in the scientific field (Yazdani, 1984). By looking at the holistic concept, using the four brain functions of thinking, feeling, perceiving in an intuitive fashion, and sensing while we synthesize them (Clark, 2007), we can contribute to the advancement of creativity.

Perceptual Development

The mounting development of brain allows enhancement in the sensory and the perceptual channels during the early school years. This is truly an age bracket in which creativity and other mental functioning can be nurtured and stabilized. Brain maturation contributes to the improvement of basic visual fine-tuning (Seifert &Huffnung, 2000). Additionally, the improvement in auditory acuity and sharpness aids the formation, transformation, storing, and recalling of sensory input in short and long-term memory. These stored materials are the basic blocks of divergent thinking, necessary to the operation of brain in production of creative and gifted thoughts. For example, the ability to distinguish sounds improves by being able to pick up sounds of the mother in the midst of a relatively noisy environment The child can differentiate the mother's voice when the T.V. is on and two conversations are taking place at the same time.

It is important to realize that many preschoolers, before age 5, have trouble focusing on shapes that are less than two feet away. By age five distance vision improves while near vision remains limited for some throughout the early school years (Seifert &Hoffnung, 2000).

Motor Development

Skill in motor development during early childhood improves tremendously. Most of the reflexes are vanished and voluntary motions are tireless. These new and energetic organisms become destine to improve their physical functioning as well as other function. Gross and fine motor skills develop to the point that preschoolers can move around fluently and utilize their hands, fingers, and large and small muscles in a surprisingly coordinated and fascinating range.

Children are capable of walking downstairs and jumping in the air with both feet at age 3.5. By age 4.5 they can run at one third adult speed, perform most sports which require running and controlling balls in a relatively semi-skillful fashion. Around age 5.5 they can balance on one foot, run a far distance without falling or swim in water for a short period of time.

As long as fine motor skills development around age 3.5, the child can copy the circle, use eating utensils, and stack several blocks on top of each other. About age 4 they can button with large buttons and copy simple geometric shapes. By age 5.5 children can use scissors to cut, draw human figures, copy simple letters and build complex structures with blocks (Kalverboer et al., 1993).

Physical Activities

All the activities during infancy and toddlerhood are divided into different age ranges due to specific characteristics of each age bracket. Maturity and capability of each stage content and structure are respected and carefully analyzed for advanced intervention and sustainability of learned materials.

Ages 3-4 Years

During this age physical activities are geared to heighten sensory awareness Two to three year old children love to try things on several occasions, no matter how impossible that might be. They have the idea that things may work out based on trial and error.

Activities to consider

Activity I. In a clear glass of clear water put some red food coloring and let the child observe it for a few seconds. Then in another clear glass of water pour yellow food coloring and let the child observe for a few seconds. Then put the red glass and yellow glass next to each other. Pour the red liquid into the yellow glass until both liquids are mixed and an orange color immerges. Ask the child to explain what happened.

Activity II. Allow the child to experience different tastes and listen to different musical notes.

Activity III. Teach the child all different colors with different shades. Provide opportunity for the child to mach colors together.

Activity IV. Come up with activities which allow the child to run, jump, and roll on the soft surfaces.

Activity V. Let the child float on the water while you are supervising the situation.

Activity VI. Ask the child to close his eyes and place a key or another simple object like a coin in his hand. While holding his hand closed, ask him to identify the object in his hand, without opening his eyes. You can place the object under the cloth and ask the child to manipulate it with his hand and tell you what the object might be. Ask the child to give you one and then two of same objects. When asking him to hand you two coins show him two fingers and say, "One and one is two," Then show the same principle with coins in front him by placing one coin next to the other and say, "One and one is two."

Ages 4-5 Years

Children between ages four and five are more selective in utilizing their senses. The physical capabilities in this age range are varied. Some children are well developed and others will reach this status later on. However, involving them in running, jumping, and other physical activities are highly recommended. Three year olds may try unsuccessfully, to pick up a heavy object, about sixty pound, several times. But four year old children will try it once, if they couldn't move the object, they will give up. Since repeating the behavior improves the skills, development of fine and gross motor abilities becomes more manageable in this age.

Activities to consider

Activity I. Encourage them to reach for objects with both hands. Then ask them to reach for the same object with left hand without involvement of right hand and vise versa.

129

Activity II. Encourage them to draw circles, straight lines, and triangles, at least 10 minutes each week with the left hand. Also, place manipulative toys at their disposal.

Activity III. Encourage them to walk, run, and jump forward and back ward

Activity V. Allow them to bend over and put their head between their legs and explain what the room looks like from that perspective.

Activity VI. With eyes closed, allow them to touch and then smell different fruits, and ask them to name the fruits.

Ages 5-6 Years

Since cognition is greatly facilitated by sensory perception, the idea of physical development contributing to recreation and play becomes a valid argument during age 4 and 6. Exposing children to outdoor activities and organized sports contributes to the physical and social development of children. Purposeful activities which have rules of conduct can shape healthy socialization. During this age range, the fine and gross motor skills are greatly improved and the biological functioning is highly diverse. This diversity allows the child to extend the physical capabilities and may create injury. Therefore, the close supervision of the child is highly recommended. On the other hand, as a parent make sure that you do not have unrealistic expectations of your child, when it comes to extent of pushing them beyond their capabilities.

Activities to consider

Activity I. Involve the child in organized sports such as soccer and baseball. The main idea is not to train a future professional, but to develop physical and recreational routines.

Activity II. Encourage them to walk and talk at the same time.

Activity III. Give them a straw and ask them to run a string through a straw with eyes open. Encourage them to do it as fast as possible and time them. Then ask them to run the string through the straw with eyes closed.

Activity IV. Ask them to give suggestions for dinner. Have them prepare the meal once a week.

Activity V. Encourage them to read on a daily basis.

Activity VI. Read a short story to the child and immediately quiz him on the story. When they are responding, they should use body movement to tell the story without using the language.

Activity VII. Teach them how to count with their fingers and show them the principle of subtraction, using their fingers.

Additional activities to consider

In this age (5 and 6), children are capable of dressing themselves, relating to representational drawings, and making jumping pattern. At this age, the child is capable of engaging in more advanced thinking known as *concrete* thinking. Physical activities which enhance coordination of mind and body are extremely beneficial in gaining and sustaining the attention.

Activities to consider

Activity I. Ask the child to close his/her eyes and listen to sounds his/her body makes, heart beat, breathing, or sniffling. Then ask him/her to reproduce the sound.

Activity II. Encourage the children to smell different flowers and then explain the smell. Make sure they give five characteristics to each smell.

Activity III. Encourage him to touch the fingers of the right hand to the left index finger, back and forth, as fast as he can, five times. Then switch the hand and use the index finger of right hand to touch the left hand fingers.

Activity IV. Allow him to close his eyes and touch the left ear with right hand and vise versa. Additionally, ask him to stand on one leg and try to hop.

Chapter Eight

COGNITIVE DEVELOPMENT IN EARLY CHILDHOOD

Cognitive Growth

This phase is known as *preoperational stage*. Piaget believes that during this stage children's use of symbolic thinking increases, mental reasoning emerges, and the use of concept increases. The progression of symbolic thinking advances cognitive ability in an array of ways (Feldman, 2007). The cognitive functioning of the children at this age uses symbols, words, images, and other signs to represent past and the present events, experiences, and concepts. Thinking in this age is rigid and inflexible, presumably because it is not grounded in action. Second, thinking in this period focuses on individual events one at the time and fails to seek the common denominators among events. Third, this fashion of thinking is not adequate for solving reasoning that requires transferring information (Brainerd, 1978). However, a great number of psychologists do not think that the cognition of the child in this age range has many limitations. Table 8.1 presents an overview of the characteristic of preoperational thought.

Characteristics	Description	Example
Animism	Assuming that all moving things are alive and have a human characteristics	The chair is happy
Egocentrism	They perceive every thing from personal view point	I'm tired, so you should be tired too.
Symbolic representation	Using symbols to represent past and present.	Look at me I am riding a horse, while sitting on the chair
Identity	Concerned with the invariance of the all-or-none and yes-or-no.	Dog is white so any white animal is dog.

Table 8.1: Characteristics of Preoperational Thoughts

One of the major elements in conceptual thinking is *classification*. This skill is also crucial in the explanation of intellect (Guilford, 1977). The position of objects in groups or categories according to some explicit standards or criteria occurs. Placement in the category is generally based on several dimensions of commonality. As the child grows older through this stage, the numbers of joint characteristics of object increases. In other words, in the beginning the child may classify several objects based on only one dimension of commonality, like the color. At the same time as the child grows older he may classify objects based on other dimensions such as size, color, values or other aspects.

One of the crucial focuses in the accelerated development of the cognitive domain in this age bracket is the excessive exposure of the children to various educational materials and not accepting the limitations that Piaget enforces on the structure of intelligence. Since the cross-sensory modalities are well developed and children are motivated to experience new circumstances, at this particular age range, collaboration between receiving channels becomes vital. For example, incorporation of audio-visual devices for introducing the educational materials can expand the intellectual capabilities of the child. Additionally, brain teasing activities and vast cultural disclosures will enhance the flexibility and originality of the creative thinking domains. More so, utilization of cross-sensory input and encouragement to use the imagination is important. Training them in imagination imagery will help developing divergent thinking skills, a crucial skill in creativity.

Cognitive Activities

The cognitive development of preschoolers, ages 3 to 6 can be characterized as preoperational (Piaget, 1975). This form of thinking is rigid, inflexible, not grounded in action, focuses on individual events, one at the time, fails to seek common ground, and is inadequate for solving logical problems (Brainerd, 1978). However, the relationship between language and thought becomes stronger through symbolism and word usage. The idea of what you see is what you think gain control and children start to use centeration to organize their thoughts in a preoperational fashion. During this phase children are more interested in seeing beyond the appearance of object and recognize that appearance can be deceiving. The symbolic function through these ages, 3-6, helps the child to realize the existence of object in the absence of presentation is possible through symbolism.

Additionally, preschoolers' cognitive functioning can be best explained by the information-processing approach (Feldman, 2007). In this approach, children can demonstrate a sophisticated understanding of numbers, memory. Recall from long-term memory is high lighted. that preschooler's perception, understanding, and memory gradually becomes more complex (Zhe & Siegler, 2001).

Age 3-4Years

During this age bracket the child is fascinated with experimenting and being involved in two person interactions. The cognitive capability of three to four year olds is filled with imaginative figures and fantasies. These children's intellectual sophistication pairs with linguistic skills and creates a fertile ground for creativity and usage of imagination. Since language becomes more sophisticated and their reasoning ability takes a new shape, children begin to consider several approaches to problem solving. To understand this reasoning we can revisit Piaget. During this *preoperational* stage, children's use of symbolic thinking grows, based on this growth, reasoning and concept formation increases (Feldman, 2007). However between ages of 2 and 4, only symbolic thinking began to associate objects with words. For example the child knows that the animal in the house which barks is called "dog" and whenever he hears barking, even if the animal is not present, the sound belongs to a dog. In other words the connection between language and thought becomes the heart of advancement in this period of cognitive growth.

Activities to consider

Activity I. Place three red balls and one white one next to each other. Then tell the child that you are going to put all red balls together. Then ask the child to repeat after you and put all the red balls together.

Activity II. Draw four circles on the piece of paper. Ask the child to count those circle. Then point to the last circle and ask the child: "what number was the last circle?"
At age 3-4, the child is hardly capable of telling you that the last circle was number 4. Repeat the process until the child gets the idea that last circle is number 4.

Activity III. Have a picture of a solid yellow cat and a picture of as solid red cat. Show the child the picture of the yellow cat and ask him/her: "What is it?" The child is supposed to recognize the cat. Then show the child the red cat and ask: "What is it?" The child may hesitate to recognize the cat because the color is different. If the child says: "cat"
Then place both pictures next to each other and ask: "What are these pictures?" Whether the child is capable of classifying or not; repeat the process several times a week. After the child gained mastery of this skill, use different objects for discrimination.

Activity IV. Start reading simple words to the child. As you pronounce the word, put your index finger under each word. Then ask the child to repeat the process. Make sure you make this activity fun and appealing. Put each learned word on the piece of paper and place it on the wall of his/her room. The placed words should be large enough for the child to be able to read it from any where in the room.

Activity V. Construct two pieces of paper with pictures of only two red balls on the first and six red balls on the other. Show both pieces of paper to the child and say: "Which one has more balls?" The child should be able to tell the correct response. If he/she did not respond correctly, you should explain.

Activity VI. Teach simultaneously, the simple mathematical principles of adding and subtracting by using fingers or blocks.

Activity VII. Encourage the child to speak in front of family about an object with which he is familiar. The child should be able to explain the object from analyzing and synthesizing perspectives. If the child is not able to carry out any of these three principles explanation, analysis, and synthesis, you need to coach the child how to utilize all three principles.

Activity VIII. Encourage the child to act like some object around the room by closing his eyes and utilizing language, while the family is together. Next, ask the child to act it out without using language.

Activity IX. Be involved with the child's preschool teacher and the child's home work

Ages 4-5 Years

During this age a gradual improvement in attention, perception, understanding, and memory reaches new heights. Due to expansion of linguistic ability and cultural context, the child becomes more symbolically oriented. This symbolic orientation aids the child to have greater long-term memory and faster information processing. The transition of information from short-term memory to long-term memory becomes more sophisticated due to a wealth of linguistic capabilities. On the other hand, the cognitive capacity of the child's mind undergoes radical change. The cognitive functioning of the child at this age receives supplementary revenues of information by being exposed to educational instructions outside of the house. Kindergarten or preschool setting opens up a new world of information and stimulation to the child. Between ages 4 to 5, the children begin to increase the complexity of their symbolic thinking by adding *organization* and *logical mental processing*. This leads to developing the idea of focusing. This logical mental processing helps children to realize that appearance can be deceiving.

One interesting aspect of cognitive development in this age bracket is incomplete understanding of transformation (Feldman, 2007). A preschool child who sees quite a few butterflies during walking in the garden may believe that a new butterfly behind the window is the same as the one who saw in the garden. The reason for that is inability to fully comprehend the notion of transformation. Transformation is very important for the development of creative thought and this age group is a perfect time to strength this ability.

Activities to consider

Activity I. Encourage reading. Provide a number of reading materials, conducive to the age of child, and ask to read the materials. You should help them learn to read. Additionally, after reading you should ask the child to explain the read materials (strengthening the comprehension skills).

Activity II. Ask the child to say the alphabet forward and back ward. Additionally, ask him to count back ward from 10 to 1.

Activity III. Teach the child the order of numbers. Draw four circles on the piece of paper. Ask the child to count those circles. Then point to the last circle and ask the child: "what number was the last circle?"(as was done at the previous age group).

Between ages 4th and 5th years of life, the child is capable of telling you that the last circle was number 4. Then point at each circle and ask: "Which circle is this one?" The child should be able to learn notion of "first", "second", "third", and "fourth."

Activity IV. Construct two pieces of paper with apicture of five dogs on the first paper and picture of six dogs on the other. Show both of them to the child and say: "Which one has more dogs?"

Activity V. Read short stories to the child and ask him/her to draw the story on the pieces of paper.

Activity VI. Teach the child to write. Start with coping, his/her first and last name. Then move to two word sentences. Each month add additional words to the sentence. Do not exceed six words per sentence during this age range.

Activity VII. Encourage the child to learn one musical instrument.

Activity VIII. Teach the child to use the computer with great degree of supervision or include all necessary safety procedures.

Activity IX. Teach the mathematical principles of adding and subtracting by using fingers, paper and pencil, and calculators.

Activity X. Encourage the child to focus on more than one aspect of an object by showing the object to the child first. Then remove the object from the child's visual field and ask the child to tell five things about the object.

Activity XI. Play school by asking the child to be a teacher and teach you the subject of his/her interest.

Activity XII. Show a child two drinking glasses of different shapes. One is short and broad; the other, tall and thin. Half-fill the short one with some colored juice. Half-fill the tall glass with the same colored juice. Show both glasses to the child and ask a question: Is there more juice in the second glass than there was in the first? You can then empty the liquid into a measuring cup to show which one has more.
The particular training in enhancing creativity should be intensifying from age 4 to six. Following are suggested activities for development of imagery, increasing the imagery pool, and incorporating the notion of imagination. Later on at between ages of 5 and six more advanced

training such as development of divergent thinking skills, imagination imagery, and creative imagination imagery will be introduced.

Activities to consider

Activity I. What would happen if you had your mouth on top of your head?
What would happen if trees had eyes?
If the rain could talk what would it say?
What if we had four hands and one leg?
Encourage the child to close his/her eyes and give you at least three answers to each question. You can encourage them to elaborate, if the child shows some interest in responding.

Activity II. Place a child in front of a fish tank and ask the child to tell you how many different ways a fish can swim?

Age 5-6 Years

In this age range children have better memory strategies. As processing speed increases, children hold more information in working memory (Hitch, Towse, & Hutton, 2001). Explicit long-term memory and implicit long-term memory will become promptly functional the routine educational exercises are very crucial to the development of creativity and giftedness. Implicit long-term memory is the learned responses, habits, and routine responses; while explicit long-term memory includes memories of specific events (Hitch, Towse, & Hutton, 2001). Also, strengthening the understanding of spoken language, expressive language, assists the child to be a divergent thinker and also helps to establish cognitive flexibility. Furthermore, as the child reaches age 6, the idea of focusing on one thought at the time and disregarding others becomes more mature. This principle is known as *centeration*, a process of concentrating on one feature of stimuli and disregarding other features. Additionally, during this age children learn that quantity is unrelated to the arrangement and physical appearance. This principle is known as *conservation*. However, a deep understanding of conservation emerges around age 7. Therefore, around age 5 and 6, the children's practice of conservation is hit-and-miss.

Another interesting development around age 5 and 6 is the emergence of intuitive thoughts (Feldman, 2007). During these ages preschoolers use primitive reasoning and usually avoid acquisition of knowledge about the world around them. This ability triggers curiosity and they try to seek out answers. When faced with the question of "why" from the child around this age, give as much detail as possible when answering. Also, encourage them to generate some more answers. Children use their intuitive ability to generate answers.

Activities to consider

Activity I. Show two pictures similar to each other with slight differences in details and ask the child to detect whether the two pictures are same or different.

Activity II. Draw a circle and ask the child to elaborate on that circle as much as possible by saying: "add as many as details to the circle." Or make this circle into something else.

Activity III. Since children are developing their implicit and explicit long-term memory a fifteen minute discussing between parent and child is important. During these meeting parents encourage the child to review events and highlights of the day in a family discussion circle.

Activity IV. During family meeting encourage the children to reflect on thoughts or habits of other people.

An Activity V. Present playing cards which is vary along more than one dimension, such as color, shape, and numbers. Then ask the child to find cards where the numbers match.

Activity VI. Learning the conservation of quantity:
Show a child two tall glasses with exactly the same amount of water in each.
As the child watches you, pour the water from one of the glasses into a wide dish.

Then, asks the child, "Is there more water in the dish or in the glass?" You are trying to find out whether the child thinks the amount of water in the dish is less or the same?"
Reason with them and make them realize that the amount of water in the tall glass and the wider dish is the same.

Activity VII. Encourage the child to read the newspaper. Then ask them to explain what they read.

Activity VIII. Persuade the child to continue improving his musical skill by practicing his favorite instrument.

Activity IX. Teach the child the mathematical principle of adding and subtracting two digits numbers without calculator and computer.

Activity X. Provide a small encyclopedia and encourage the child to read a page a day and then talk about it in the family meeting.

Activity XI. Encourage the child to work on a manuscript and use family members to perform the script, with the child as a director.

Activity XII. Be involved with child's preschool teacher

Activity XIII. Play school by asking the child to be a teacher and teach you the subject of his/her interest.

Originality and Imagery

Originality is one of the essential components of creativity. Originality means uniqueness. One of the qualities of creative thought is originality and novelty (Torrance, 1962). The following activities are designed to enhance creativity via originality. Since imagination imagery plays a very vital role in the development of *originality*, one of the characteristics of creative thought. Facilitation of this skill will promote inventiveness.

Activities to consider

Activity I. Expose a child to a series of classical music for five minutes, while their eyes are shut. Then ask them to play the sound back in their mind and try to explain what their heard. This improves their verbal pool through formation of imagery.

Activity II. With the eyes closed, ask the child to imagine a dog is sniffing around the kitchen. Then ask the child to find out what the dog sees, smells, and hears. Encourage a child to make a story and reflect the dog's behaviors around the kitchen.

Activity III. Ask the child to imagine a book, any book. Ask the child to start changing things about the image of that book in their mind. Then ask the child to explain the new product of his/ imagination. Your final goal for this exercise is to encourage the child to redefine the physical and logical purpose of that book.

Chapter Nine

EMOTIONAL DEVELOPMENT IN EARLY CHILDHOOD

Emotional Growth

Emotion affects every part of human functioning. In addition to feeling and sentiment, emotion supports and also provides a gateway to cognitive processing and enhances or inhibits higher cognitive functioning (Clark, 2007). Preschoolers are at an appealing juncture—too old to hang onto adults every moment but too young to run off with age-mates ((Poole, Warren, & Nunez, 2007). Young ones have instinctively resolved this dilemma by simply watching older children play. If we ask a preschooler, particularly between the ages 3 to 5 what makes them different from other kids, they reply with an answer like, "I am boy", "I have a long hair", or "I can ride my bicycle." Such responses indicate self-concept or their *identity*. In other words they have sets of beliefs about themselves and identify themselves then. One of the hallmarks of emotional development in preschoolers is the optimistic view held about them. The main reason for such a view is that they have not yet started to compare themselves with others (Feldman, 2007). However, preschoolers display the full range of human emotions in excess of 200 times a day in a multiplicity of techniques and presentations (Stein, 2002).

Different psychological schools of thought view differently the importance of early childhood. Freud believes that majority of human personality forms within first five years of life. From the behavioral stand point, most of our early social learning takes place in the context of home and early environments through modeling, reinforcing, and association.

Erick Erikson introduced a theory, known as *psychosocial development*, which emphasizes the interaction of individuals with others. In this theory Erikson highlights the challenges of society and culture on shaping our development. He believes that we go through 8 distinct stages of development from birth to death. Table 9.1 shows a summary of Erikson's stages of psychosocial development. With regard to the preschoolers, Erikson suggested that children between ages 2 to the end of sixth years go through two stages of psychosocial developmental. *Autonomy versus shame and doubt* and *initiative versus guilt.*

At age two the children are involved with focusing on the crisis of *autonomy versus shame and doubt.* In this phase of psychosocial development, which generally concludes at age three, children develop the ability to balance their own

Stage	Approximate Age	Constructive Effect
1. Trust-versus-mistrust	Birth-1.5 years	Feeling of trust and support
2. Autonomy-versus shame and doubt	1.5-3 years	Self-adequacy and explanatory mode
3. Initiative-versus-guilt	3-6	Developing the sense of discovery
4. Industry-versus-inferiority	6-12	Development of self-confidence
5. Identity-versus-confusion	Adolescence	Alertness of uniqueness of self
6. Intimacy-versus-isolation	Early adulthood	Development of love, close relationships, and sexual relationships
7. Generativity-versus-stagnation	Middle adulthood	Sense of contribution to permanence of life
8. Ego integrity-versus- despair	Late adulthood	Sense of achievement and unity in life

Table 9.1 a summary of Erikson psychosocial stages

demands with of self control. This process of self-control is a two sided coin. On the autonomy side the factor of control seeks independence intended at bodily, social, and psychological functioning. This leads to the further development of the *will*. On the other side of this coin is the issue of shame and doubt. This involves a loss of self-respect due to failure to meet one's own standards (Lewis, 1992).

The third of Erikson's stages of psychosocial development for this age bracket is known as *initiative verse guilt*. In this stage of psychosocial development children between ages three to six try to merge autonomy with the ability to explore new activities and ideas and to decisively pursue and achieve tasks and goals (Seifert & Hoffnung, 2000). If failure arises in pursuing such goals, the result will be self-criticism and not living up to the parent's expectation. This self-criticism has a utility to make the child feel guilty. This crisis often happens when the child engages on physical or emotional situations more than he/she can handle. If during this crisis phase the children were helped and accepted, they develop the virtue of *purpose*. Based on these two phases of psychosocial development, issues such as relationship with parents, siblings, and friend takes more constrictive role in navigating through this crisis.

Another important issue in this age bracket which influences the personality of the child is pro-social behaviors. These behaviors, empathy and acceptance in the conflict and aggression state of affairs, help the child to sort out the differences which appear in the play patterns. Playing is a social activity which teaches the child many different skills such as physical, cognitive, and psychosocial in particular. Since playing dominates the preschool area, engaging in play becomes an important vehicle for social interaction and social and interpersonal skills building.

The Emergence of the Theory of Mind

What features are riveted in the emergence of the theory of the mind? During preschool years, children develop more emotional capability regarding self-awareness. One of the fundamental alleys in this development is the expansion of language and utilization of symbolic implication. The increasing level of sophistication in usage of language opens the door for children's theory of the mind. The wealth of social engagement, cultural influence, and play indicates how children view their opinions about themselves and what others' actions mean, other's perspective.

The curiosity of children about the nature of the mind opens a door to an understanding of their own mental processing as well others. Studies of the theory of the mind view the child as "a thinker who is trying to explain, predict, and understand people's thoughts, feelings, and actions" (Harris, 2006). Children around age three begin to understand three concepts in regard to the theory of the mind. First, the child realizes that the person can perceive an object from the person's personal perspective. In other words, the child may see an object in his/her way but the others may see the same object in their way. Second, the child can differentiate between positive emotions, "happiness" and negative emotions, "sadness". Third, the child recognizes that others have the desire to get what they want.

As the child grows older, the theory of the mind and understanding of the child from the notion of the mind grows. Around age 4 and 5 the child understands that the mind can signify reality precisely or inaccurately, *false belief* (Wellman, Cross, & Watson, 2001). This indicates that a deeper understanding of the mind in children before age six is limited only to the understanding of the timing of mental events. After age six, the concept of mind becomes more complex and the understanding of the mind expands to the *mental status*. In this period, children realize that familiar items are easier to learn than unfamiliar ones. The key to expanding creativity in preschoolers is making their environment rich with different stimulations and encouraging and providing opportunities to experience more diverse knowledge.

Moral Development

The second year of life is characterized the beginning of communication, shifting to symbolic understanding, independent mobilization, and innocently questioning the environment. Preschool phase is the crucial commencement for moral, ethical, and psychosocial development. Values, norms, and standards are usually formed through modeling and social contacts throughout the life span. But early childhood has a profound impact on the accumulation of such norms and standards of ethical and moral development. The reason for the importance of this age range is the idea that preschoolers are too old to hang onto adults every moments but too young to run off with age-mates ((Poole, Warren, & Nunez, 2007).

Granting the fact that learning does not take place in a vacuum; an important factors to bear in mind: *social learning and modeling*. As a parent or caregiver, our role is diversely affected by culture, social and ethical standards, and personal faith and beliefs. Motivating the child to learn these values, norms, and standards is significantly important during this age.

Though moral development starts at an older age, psychologists are mostly in agreement that moral development and symbolic thinking has logical relationships. To explain morality, the issue of conscience and its development should be explained. As a toddler, the child forms the internal framework that evaluates all of the external behaviors and responses. Philosophically there are three views of moral development (Sutton-Smith, 1973):

1. *Innate Purity*: Child arrives in the world as a morally pure being and all the changes are the product of environment.
2. *Original Sin*: A child arrives in the world with evil instinct and impulses and it is the social responsibility to modify these impulses.
3. *Tabula Rasa* (Blank slate): The child comes to this world neither good nor bad (Hoffman, 1970). But society determines the behavior and judges it based on its standards.

Selman, explained morality in two stages reasoning: *moral realism or Heteronymous morality* or *moral reciprocity* and *Autonomous morality* (Selman, 1980).

Heteronymous morality or moral realism is inflexible and concrete. Children think that rules are absolute, fixed, and unchangeable. If you break it, punishment will inescapably follow. Based on moral realism, this juncture manifests between age three to six. Consequently, autonomous morality or morality of reciprocity needs to be flexible in order to provide equilibrium in human interactions. After age six or seven, children accept social rules but see them as more arbitrary and changeable than fixed and absolute regulations.

Another psychologist who worked very diligently in the field of moral development is Kohlberg. In his theory the value of law and society are well defined and based on *"what is right and what is wrong."* Following are the three major stages of moral developments (Kohlberg, 1976): preconvention morality, conventional morality, and post conventional morality. In the preconvention morality paradigm children conform to rules in order to gain rewards and avoid punishment. Therefore, moral decisions are based on consequences of an act, not intentionality. On the other hand, in the conventional morality pattern children attempt to be recognized or obey rules to win a prize. The gain in practicing such a modality is being recognized and maintaining social order. In post conventional morality, the individual recognizes that rules are necessary but it can be flexible. Based on some circumstances, the universal principle can over rule the established structure. Figure 9.2 shows the Kohlberg's moral developmental stages:

Pre-convention morality	A.	Punishment and obedience: child decides what is wrong based on what is punished. Obedience is based on avoiding the punishment.
	B.	Child follows rules based on what is on one's immediate interest. The child does good things because of reciprocity. You do for me, I do it for you.
Conventional morality	A.	Being good. The child does things because he wants to be known as he a "good boy or a good girl". The child loyalty, trust, and respect by keeping mutual relationship.
Conventional morality	B.	The child shifts his focus from family to others. Good, is fulfilling duties and following the "law" of the society. The child does things because it is the law.

| Post-conventional or principle morality | A. | Humans acts to achieve the greatest good. The child after age five is aware that there are different values and views about things which can be circumstantial. Though laws are needed, they are subject to change too for greater good of society. |
| | B. | Humans develops sets of principles, which are self-chosen and ethical. The core of beliefs at this level is an understanding between "law" and "conscience". In this level, conscience dominates everything's. |

Figure 9.2 Kohlberg's moral developmental stages

Children can demonstrate amazing abilities in moral development absorbing behaviors of adult around them. Half a century ago, scientists did not dare to acknowledge such potential. Enriching the growth and development of children in early age can enhance their chances to be happy and successful being in life. They not only bring fulfillment to themselves but they also can make this world a better place for all of us.

Emotional Activities

Age 3-4 Years

In this age bracket, forming a sense of *self* becomes a crucial factor in the preschooler's psychosocial development. In this period the child becomes aware of his/her identity, separate from others and tries to regulate it as much as possible. Unfortunately, the tool to succeed is not naturally available. In this case the caregiver can help to develop these skills and aids in formation of self-identity.

The self-concept or the child's identity consists of sets of beliefs about what they are like as individuals (Marsh, Ellis, & Craven, 2002). For example, if the child was asked to specify what makes him/her different from other kids, he/she would respond: "I am a good jumper." Or "I like to soup."According to Erikson (1963), the children between the ages of 3 to 6 go through a phase known as *initiative—versus-guilt*. Throughout this phase, children face conflicts between the desire to act independently from their parents and guilt that comes from the failure when they don't succeed. The caregiver should provide the child opportunities to act self-reliantly, while still giving him directions (Feldman, 2007). However, around age 3 to 4, the preschooler has better control of their temptation and more influent to give themselves direction. In other words they have a capability to regulate self. Since mastery over bodily functioning helps the crisis of autonomy versus shame, the child should be encourages to take over the responsibility of these functions.

Another social development at this age is the development of friendships. The goals and outcomes gained from this friendship are different than those of parents and caregivers. Friendships with parents bring protection, direction and care. But relationship with friends brings companionship, fun and play.

Perhaps one of the most fascinating activities for 3 to 4 year olds is play. As we discussed in chapter four, play can be a great instrument to develop all areas of growth and development. For three year olds play is aimed at just doing something for the sake of being active. Achieving an end product is not the goal of this kind of play (Bober, Humphry, & Carswell, 2001). This kind of play is known as *functional play* and includes simple, repetitive activities. As the child reaches age four this functional play changes to a kind of play that is more complex. At this age, the child begins to manipulate objects that he/she plays with, aimed at making something out of that objects; the child has definitive goals. This kind of play is known as constructive play, such as making a house out of blocks. This particular mode of play is essential in developing creative abilities.

Activities to Consider

Activity I. Encourage the child to set meal time. This allows the child to learn decision-making skills.

Activity II. Provide blocks and toys that the child could build structure.

Activity III. Encourage independent hygiene skills (toileting, brushing teeth, and getting dress).

Activity IV. Have a daily meeting with the child in a quiet place. Go over child activities and reinforce him/her for all of the right decisions he made. Be supportive but truthful about it.

Activity V. Allow the child to criticize unjust situations at home,

Activity VI. Encourage the child to use his/her imagination during make believe story telling or play.

Activity VII. Encourage the child to make decisions in many activities during the day and talk about the consequences of their decision.

Age 4-5 Years

This age bracket is the beginning of a new developmental stage of *initiative versus guilt*. In this stage the child is interested to achieving greater mastery and responsibility. This stage lasts from age four to the end of six. Therefore all of the activities should reinforce each other during the age bracket 4-5 and 5-6. Since imagination plays a vital role in cognitive functioning of the child during this age bracket. Parents, counselors, and educators should realize that some of the imaginative responses may not produce results. Therefore, there is a cautionary factor here, needed to be considered. The result of fantasy should be respected and allowed to be expressed without judgment. This balance creates a protection against feeling of guilt and encourages initiative.

One of the instrumental skills in developing creativity around this age is the development of a sense of racial identity and gender. Preschoolers structure racial outlook mainly in response to their environment, including parents and other influences. The more universally oriented practices introduced during this early age, the more openness toward world citizenship develops. Additionally, avoidance from gender-oriented stereotypes helps brighten the horizon of the child. Though gender differences emerge during early childhood, the expectation of the gender role can be hindering in the development of creativity.

Different theories look at gender identity in different ways. In a psychoanalytic approach a framework of gender identity is based on the subconscious and physiological assignments. In social learning theories, the idea of learning through modeling and environmental influences plays an important role in gender identity. In pure behaviorism the idea of reinforcing the response or conditioning the stimuli to change the behavior become the criteria for manifestation of gender identity related behaviors.

Additionally, play, social relations, and discipline are among the important factors in shaping the personality of preschoolers. Perhaps one of the crucial factors is the type of parenting, (see table 9.3). Four major parenting styles were identified by Baumrind (1971, 1981) and later updated by Maccoby and Martin (1983). The method of approaching the child's needs and the configuration of the parents' personalities gives a direction in unlocking creative ability. Additionally, these factors play an important role in formation of child's personality.

In this age stage, 4-5, the child begins to include an authentic friendship, which involves trust (Feldman, 2007). They become more engage in constructive and associative plays. Depending on what style of discipline the parents deploy, the child become responsive or nonresponsive to the notion of discipline. These factors are critical in the child's responses to discipline: the degree of parental involvement, emotional attachment, friendship between child and parent, and respect for dependency.

Types of parenting	Characteristics
Authoritarian	Controlling, rigid, cold, punitive, demand obedience,
Permissive	Lax and inconsistent, require little from children, less responsibility, limited control

| Authoritative | Firm, setting clear boundaries and limits, relatively strict, emotionally supportive, communication open, and reason with the child |
| Uninvolved | Display indifference, rejecting behavior, detached emotionally, Just provides food and clothing (basic needs) |

Table 9.3 Parenting Styles

Activity I. Assign some simple choruses for the child that he/she can perform without failure.

Activity II. Discuss the success of these choruses with other family members and let the child know that he/she is capable and good at it.

Activity III. Increase the degree of difficulty of the choruses through time. But be mindful of the ideas so you are preventing failure.

Activity IV. Teach the child to clarify the feeling of self.

Activity V. Exercise "sorting out the feelings". *Sorting out the feeling* is a game the child plays with parents. Children are asked to demonstrate three different feelings: joy, sadness, and empathy. The children is supposed to use facial expression, body language, and explanation of these feelings.

Activity VI. Ask the child to explain the impact of sorting out the feeling game on one of the family members, on trees; and on pet.

Age 5-6 Years

In this age range the child is exposed to two different environments, home and preschool. The need for consistency between these two environments is indispensable. Children may start to experience some anxiety from high expectations. To ease these feelings parents should be supportive, nonjudgmental, and resourceful. By now, the child is already functioning within creative or giftedness range and respecting the child's judgment is essential to the mental health of the child. Since the next stage of psychosocial development is mastery and competency in what they like To do, a calm and compassionate environment becomes necessary

Activity I. Encourage children to become involved with expression of their emotions by miming several feelings such as joy, anger, wonder, and sadness.

Activity II. Encourage the child to clarify awareness of the needs and feelings of Other people member of family (Clark, 2007).

Activity III. Ask the child to verbalize your expectations of others after you show them magazine pictures of people with different facial and emotional expressions. You can act out different feelings through play and ask the child to name, and clarify the feeling and the consequences of such a feeling on you as a performer and a child as an observer.

Activity IV. Engage the child in voluntary work around the house.

Activity V. Give the child a series of chores to do around the house. Give positive feedback to the child regarding the activities.

Activity VI. Develop a family circle and listen to the feelings of each other, while involving the child.

Activity VII. Have discussions about moral issues, particularly encouraging the child to do things for the sake of doing good. The child should realize that his/ her rights are as important as others rights.

Activity VIII. Encourage the child to engage with discussions with group of adults or intellectual peers (Clark, 2007).

Activity IX. Encourage and collaborate with the child in developing realistic goals settings about simple or relatively complex affairs of the house.

Other members of family should be involved in all of the group activities. Father as well as mother should be involved with these activities.

Early Education and Beyond

Stimulation of creative ability, in the early years of life opens the door for a happier and more successful individual. The pleasure of meaningful, relaxed, and spiritually lifted life can make this world a better place to live. However, the implication of influential curriculum for children beyond the age of 6 ought to be favorably considered.

The impact of quality early education serves to increase the quality and quantity of human thinking ability. The known components of cognition can be nurtured by the *Influential Curriculum* (IC). The Influential Curriculum's design should be developed based on the individual's stages of developmental.

Orchestrating early intervention through IC requires skill and competence. To optimally achieve the objectives for empowering the cognitive domain, IC is designed to enhance: the speed and quality of information transformed from receiving organ to short term memory and ultimately to the long-term memory; and, decision-making ability, through utilizing fluency, flexibility, and originality. In empowering the emotional domain, IC is intended to diversify drive, socialization and interpersonal relations, and concept of the self.

REFRENCES

Adams, R. J., & Courage, M. L. (1998). Development of chromatic discrimination In early infancy. *Behavioral brain Research, 67,* 99-101.

Adams, R. D., & Victor, M.(1989). *Principle of neurology* (4th Ed.). New York: McGrew-Hill.

Ainsworth, M. S., & Bowlby, J. (1991). An ethological approach to personality development. *American Psychologist, 46,* 333-341.

Adler, A. (1956). *The individual psychology of Alfred Adler.* New York: Basic Books

Amabilie, T. M. (1996). *Creativity in context: Update to "The social psychology of Creativity."* Boulder, CO: Westview

American Psychiatric Association. (2000). *Diagnostic and statistical manual of mental disorders*—IV-TR. Washington, D.C.: Author.

Baumrind, D. (1971). Current pattern of parental authority. *Developmental Psychology Monographs, 4*(1, Pt. 2).

Baumrind, D. (1980). New direction in socialization research, *Psychological Bulletin, 35* 639-652.

Bee, H & Boyd, D. A.. (2009).*The developing child* (12th ed). New York: Harper & row publisher

Berk, L, E. (2006). *Child Development* (7th ed.) New York: Pearson

Berlyne, D. E. (1960).*Conflict, arousal and curiosity*, New York: McGraw-Hill.

Blakeslee, T. R. (1937). *The right brain: A new understanding of unconscious mind and Its creative power.* New York: Anchor Press.

Brainerd, C. J., (1978). *Piaget's theory of intelligence.* New Jersey: Prentice-Hall

Bober, S. Humphry, R. & Carswell, H. (2001). Toddler's persistence in the emerging Occupations of functional play and self-feeding. *American Journal of Occupational Therapy, 55,* 369-376.

Bowlby, J. (1969). *Attachment and loss: Vol. 1. Attachment.* New York: Basic Books

Brownfield, C. A. (1965). *Isolation: Clinical and experimental approaches.* New York: Alfred A. Knopf.

Brained, C. J. (1978). *Piaget theory of intelligence.* Englewood, CA: Prentice-Hall Inc..

Brainerd, C. J. (1978). Learning research and Piagtian theory. In L.S. Siegel & C. J. Brainerd (Eds). *Alternative to Piaget: Critical essay on the theory.* New York: Academic Press.

Bruner, J. (1968). *Process of cognitive growth: infancy.* Worcerester, Mass: ClarkUniversity Press.

Cernoch, J., & Porter, R. (1985). Recognition of maternal auxiliary odors by infants. *Child Development, 56,* 1593-1598.

Chase, S., & Thomas, A. (1986). *Temperament in clinical practice.* New York: Guilford

Clark, B. (2007). *Growing up gifted*, 7th ed. Saddle River NJ: Prentice Hall Publishing Company.

Clifton, R. K., Rochat, P., Robin, D. J., & Berthier, N. E. (1994). Multimodal Perception in the control of infant reaching. *Journal of Experimental Psychology: Human perception and performance*, 20, 867-886.

Craig, G. J. & Dunn, W. L. (2007). Understanding Human Development. Upper Saddler River, NJ: Pearson Prentice Hall.

Cowart B, J. (1981). Development of taste perception in human: sensitivity and Performance throughout the life span. *Psychological bulletin*, 90, 40-43.

Cunningham, B. (1993). Child Development, New York: Harper Collins.

Ebbs, J. H., Tisdall, F. F., & Scott, W. A. (1942). *The influence of parental diet on Mother and child.* Millbank Memorial Fun Quart.

Eccles, J. C. (1973). The physiology of imagination, in W. H. Freeman (Ed), *Scientific American resource Library: Reading in psychology,* Washington, D. C.: Scientific American.

Edwards, C. P., & Hiler, C. (1993). *A Teacher's Guide to Exhibit: The Hundred Languages of Children.* Lexington, KY: College of Human Environmental Sciences, University of Kentucky.

Eisenberg, A. Murkoff, H. E., & Hathaway, S. E. (1989). *What to expect the first year.* New York: Workman.

Eisenberg, A, Murkoff, H. E., & Hathaway, S. E. (1989). *What to expect when you're expecting.* New York: Workman.

Erikson, E. H. (1950). *Childhood and society.* New York: Norton.

Erikson, E. H. (1968). *Identity and the life cycle*. New York: Norton.

Erikson, E. H. (1982). *The life cycle completed: A review*. New York: Norton.

Feldman, R. S. (2007). *Child Development (4ᵗʰ, Ed.)*.Upper Saddle River, NJ: Pearson

Ferguson, M.(1973). *The brain revolution*. New York: Taplinger.

Flechsig, P. E.. (1920). *Anatomie des menschilchen Gehirns und Ruckenmarks auf Myelogenestischer*. Liepzig: G thieme.

Forisha, B. D. (1975). Mental imagery and verbal processes: A developmental study. *Developmental psychology*, 11, 259-267.

Freud, S. (1930). *Civilization and its discontent*. New York: Norton.

Freund, H., Sabel, B., & Witte, O. (Eds) (1997). *Brain plasticity*. Philadelphia: Lippicott-Raven

Frijda, N. (2000).The psychologist's point of view. In M. Lewis & J. M. Haviland-Jones (Eds.). Handbook of *emotions* (pp.59-74). New York: Guilford

Fromm, E. (1959). *Creative and its cultivation*. The creative attitude. In H. H. Anderson, New York: Harper & Row

Gibson, E. J. (2000). Perceptual learning in development: Some basic concept, *Ecological Psychology*, 12, 295-302.

Glover, J. A., Bruning, H., & Filbeck, R. W. (1983). *Educational Psychology: Principles and Application*. Boston. MA: Little, Brown and Company.

Gordon, W., (1961). *Synetics: The development of creative capacity*. New York: Harper & Row.

Gowan J., C., (1978). Incubation, imagery, and creativity. *Journal of Mental Imagery*, 2 (1), 23-32.

Greenspan, S.I. (1991) Clinical assessment of emotional milestone in infancy and early childhood. *Pediatric clinic of north America*, vol. 38. No. 6, December,

Guilford, J. P. (1976).*The nature of human intelligence*. New York: McGraw-Hill.

Guilford, J. P. (1977). *Way beyond I.Q.* Buffalo, New York: Creative foundation Press.

Gwiazad, J. & Brich, E. E. (2001). Perceptual development: Vision. In E. B. (Goldstein (Ed.), *Blackwell handbook of perception* (pp.636-668). Malden, MA: Blackwell.

Hagen, J. & Clark, B. (1977). *Unusual capacity-unusual needs*. Paper presented at second Conference of the World Council for Gifted, San Francisco.

Hall, C. S., & Lindzey, G. (1985). *Introduction to theories of personality*. New York: Wiley.

Halle, T. G. (2003). Emotional development and well-being. IN M. H. Bornstein. L. Davidson, C. I..M, Keys, K. A. Moore, & The center of the child well-being: Positive Development across the life course (pp. 125-138). Mahwah NJ: Erlbaum.

Harris, P. L. (2006). Social cognition. In W. Damon & R. Lerner (Eds.), *Handbook of Child Psychology* (6th ed.) New York: Wiley.

Hitch, G. J., Towse, J. N., & Hutton, U. (2001). What limits children's working memory Span? Theoretical accounts and applications for scholastic development, *Journal of Experimental Psychology: General, 130*, 184-198.

Hoffman, M. L. Moral development. (1970). In P. H Mussen (Ed.), *Carmichael's manual of child psychology*. Vol. II. New York: Wiley.

Holyoak, K., & Thagard,P. (1995). *Mental laps: Analogy in creative thoughts*. Cambridge, MA: MIT Press/Bradford Books

Isen, A., & Reeves, J. (2005). The influence of positive affect on intrinsic and extrinsic motivation. Facilitating enjoyment of play, responsible work behavior, and self control. *Motivation and Emotion, 29,* 297-325.

Izard, C. E. (1994). Inmate and universal facial expressions: Evidence from Developmental and cross cultural research. *Psychological Bulletin, 115,* 288-299.

James W. (1890). *The principle of psychology*. New York: Holt.

Jung, C. G. (1916). *Analytical psychology*. New York: Moffat, Yard.

Jung, C. G. (1964). (Ed.). *Man and his symbols*. New York: Dell.

Kalverboer, A., Hopkins, B. & Gouze, R (Eds.). (1993).*Motor development in early and late childhood.* New York: Cambridge University Press.

Khatena, J. (1973a). Imagination imagery by children and production of analogy. *Gifted Child quarterly,* 17, (2). 98-102.

Khatena, J. (1978). Frontiers of creative imagination imagery, *Journal of Mental, Imagery,*2 33-46.

Khatena, J. (1979) *Teaching gifted children to use creative imagination imagery*. Starkville, MS.: Allen associates.

Khatena J. (1980). *Creative imagination imagery, Action Book.* Starkville, MS: Allen Associate.

Khatena, J. (1982). *The educational psychology of gifted*. New York: John Wiley & son,

Klahr, D., & Simon, H. A. (1999). Studies of scientific discovery: Complementary approaches and convergent findings. *Psychological Bulletin, 125*, 524-543.

Klaus, H. M. & Kennell, J. H. (1976). *Maternal-infant bonding*. St. Louis: Mosby.

Kochanska, G., Coy, K. C.., Tjebkes, T. I., & Husarek, S. J. (1998). Individual Differences in emotionality in infancy. Child Development, 64. 375-390

Lewis, M. (1992). Shame: *The exposed self*. New York: The free press.

Maccoby, E. E., & Martin, J. A. (1983). Socialization in the context of family: Parent child interaction. In P. H. Mussen (Ed.) & E. M. Hetherington (Vol. Ed.) *Handbook of child psychology: Vol. 4. Socialization, personality, and social development (4ᵗʰ ed.*, pp. 1-101). New York: Wiley.

Marsh, H.., Ellis, L., & Carven, R. (2002). How do preschool children feel about themselves? Unraveling measurement and multidimensional self-concept structure. *Developmental Psychology,38*, 376-393.

Maslow, A. (1954). Motivation and personality. New York: Harper & Row.

Murray, P. (1989). *Genius: The history of an idea*. Oxford, UK: Blackwell.

Nelson, C. A., Thomas, K., & de Hann, M. (2006). Neural bases of cognitive development. In W. Damon & R. M. Lerner (Series Eds.), handbook of child psychology: Vol. 2. cognition, perception, and language (6ᵗʰ ed., pp3-57). Hoboken, NJ: Wiley.

Nihart, M. A. (1993). Growth and development of brain. *Journal of Child and Adolescent Psychiatry and Mental Health Nursing, 6,* 39-40.

Neukrug, E. S., & Fawcett, C, R. (2006). *Essential of testing and assessment: A practical Guide for counselors, social workers, and psychologists.* Belmont, CA: Thomson Higher Education.

Ohlsson, S. (1992). Information-processing explanations of insight and related Phenomenon. In M. T. Kenne & K. J. Gilhooly (Eds.), *Advances in psychology of Thinking* (Vol. 1. pp. 1-44). New York: Harvester Wheatsheaf.

Piaget, J. (1975). *The development of thoughts: Equilibration of cognitive structures.* New York: Viking press.

Piechowski, M. M. (1989). Developmental potential and growth of self. In J. Van Tassel-Baska & P. Olszewski-Kubilius (Eds.), *Pattern of influence on gifted Learners: The home, the self, and the school* (pp. 87-101). New York: Teachers College Press. (Question from unabridged version, available from author, Northland College, Ashland, WI).

Pool, D., Warren, A., & Nunez, N. (2007). *The story of human development.* New Jersey: Pearson Education INC.

Renzulli, J. (1978). "What makes giftedness?" Reexamining the definition. *Phi Delta Kappan, 60,* 180-184; 261.

Richardson, A. (1969). *Mental imagery.* New York: Spring Publishing.

Rochat, P., Goubet, N., & Sanders, S. J. (1999). To reach or not top reach? Perception Of body effectiveness by young infants. *Infant and Child Development,8,* 129-148.

Rosenweig, M. (1996). Environmental complexity, cerebral change and behavior *American Psychologist,* 21, 321-332.

Roskinski, R. R. (1977). The development of visual perception. Santa Monica, CA: Goodyear

Sagan, c. (1977). *The dragons of Eden*. New York: Random house,.

Salapatek, P., & Kessen, W. Visual (1966). Scanning of triangles by human newborn. *J. exp. Child psychology* 3, 113-122.

Sattler, J. M. (1988). *Assessment of children*. San Diego, CA: Jerome Sattler, Publisher.

Sattler, J. M. (2004). Assessment of Children WISC-IV and WPPSI-III supplement San Diego, CA: Jerome Sattler, Publisher.

Sellin, D., Birch, J. (1980). *Educating gifted and talented learners*. Rockville, MD: An Aspen Publishing.

Seifert, K. L., &Hoffnung, R. L. (2000). Child and adolescent development. Boston MA: Houghton Mifflin Compony.

Selman, R. L. (1980).*The growth of interpersonal understanding*. New York: Academic Press,.

Seilel, H., Rosenstein, B., & Pathak, A. (Eds). (1997). *Primary care of the newborn (2nd^{e}d.)* St. Louis: Mosby.

Silverman, L K. (2000). *Counseling the gifted & talented*. Denver, CO: Love publishing Company.

Simon, H. A. (1986). The information-processing explanation of Gestalt phenomena. *Computers in Human Behavior, 2*, 241-255.

Simonton, D. K. (1999). Origins of genius: Darwin perspective on creativity. New York: Oxford.

Slater, A., Bremner, G., Johnson, S. P., Shaerwood, P., Hayes, R., & Brown, E. (2000). Newborn infants' preference for attentive faces: The role of internal and external facial features. *Infancy, 1*, 265-274.

Snow, C. W. (1998). Infant development. Upper Saddler River, NJ: Prentice Hall.

Sperry, R. W. (1968). Hemisphere deconnection and unit of conscious awareness. *American Psychologist, 23*, 723-733.

Stein, N. L. (2002). Memories foe emotional stressful and traumatic events. In J. M. Mandler, N. L. Stein, P. J. Bauer, & M. Robinowitz (Ed.), *Representation, memory, and development: Essays in honor of Jean Mandler* (pp.247-265). Mahwah, NJ: Erlbaum.

Steiner, J. E., (1979). Human facial expression in response to taste and smell stimulation. In H. W. Reese & L, P. Lipsitt (Eds.), *Advances in child development and behavior* (vol. 13, pp.257-295). New York: Academic Press.

Sternberg, R. J. (1997b). *Successful intelligence: How practical and creative intelligence Determine success in life.* New York: Plume

Sternberg, R. J., Kaufman, J. C., & Pretz, J. E. (2002). *The creativity countdown.* Hove, England: Psychology Press.

Sternberg, R. L., & Lubart, T. L. (1996). Investing creativity. *American Psychologist, 51*, 677-688.

Stipek, D. J., Gralinski, H., & Kopp, C. B. (1990). Self-concept developt in the toddler years. *Developmental psychology, 26*, 972-977.

Sutton-Smith, B., (1973). *Child psychology,* New York: Appleton-century-craft,.

Teller, D. Y. (1998). Spatial and temporal aspects of infant color vision. Proceedings of the International Color Vision Society. *Vision Research, 38*(21), 3275-3282.

Terman, L(1947). Mental and physical trades of thousands gifted children. In L. Terman (Ed.), *Genetic studies of genius* (vol. I). Stanford: Stanford University Press,

Teyler, T.(1977). An introduction to neuroscience. In M. Wittrock (ed.), *The human brain*. Englewood Cliffs, NJ.: Prentice-Hall.

Thomas, A., & Chess, S. (1977). *Temperament and development*. New York: Brunner/Mazel,

Torrance, E. P. (1962). *Guiding creative talent*. Englewood cliffs, NJ.: Prentice-Hall,

Verny, T. (1981). *The secret life of the unborn child*. New York: Summit books.

Wallas, G. (1926). The art of thought. London: Cape

Weisberg, R. W. (1995). Prolegomena to theories of insight in problem solving: Definition of terms and taxonomy of problems. In R. J. Sternberg & J, E. Davidson (Eds.), *The nature of insight* (pp. 157-196). Cambridge, MA: MIT Press.

Weisberg, R. W. (2006). Creativity: Understanding Innovation in Problem Solving, Science, Invention, and the Art New Jersey: John Wiley & Sons

Wellman, H. M., Cross, D., & Watson, J. (2001). Meta-analysis of theory-of-mind Development: The truth about false belief. *Child Development, 72*, 655-684.

Wittrock, M. (1980). Learning and the brain. In M. Wittrock (Ed.), *The brain and Psychology*. New York: Academic Press

Yazdani, N. N., (1984). *The effect of audio-visual interferences on hemispheric function in production of original verbal imagery*. Starkville MS.

Zhe, C., & Siegler, R. S. (2000). Across the Great Divide: Bridging the gap between Understanding of toddlers' and older children's thinking, *Monographs of the Society For Research in Child Development,* 65(2, Serial No. 261).

A concise-yet satisfying-guide to the basic of development of creativity and giftedness

Designed specifically for practicing helping professionals, educators, and parents, Dr. Nanolla Yazdani's *Promoting Creativity in Childhood* offers a broad overview of founding principles and practical approaches for developing creative potential of children at school and at home. Though brief, this pragmatic text provides all the materials suggested by accrediting bodies for basic guidance, teaching, and developing courses. *Promoting Creativity in Childhood* offers insight into an array of important topics, including:

- The history of child developmental
- Prenatal and postnatal development
- The nature, dynamics, and stimulation of creativity and imagination imagery
- Physical, cognitive, and psychosocial creativity development from embryonic stages to the conclusion of sixth year of life.
- The role of play
- Basics for parents, developing curriculum in classroom, and interacting with children at home

This state-of-the art text provides developmental activities intended to enhance children's creativity and enrich their developmental journey